Harold Fehderau

DEC - - 1976

GRAMMAR DISCOVERY PROCEDURES

JANUA LINGUARUM

STUDIA MEMORIAE
NICOLAI VAN WIJK DEDICATA

edenda curat

C. H. VAN SCHOONEVELD

INDIANA UNIVERSITY

SERIES MINOR
NR. XXXIII

1973

MOUTON

THE HAGUE · PARIS

GRAMMAR DISCOVERY PROCEDURES

A FIELD MANUAL

by

ROBERT E. LONGACRE

SUMMER INSTITUTE OF LINGUISTICS

Third Printing

1973

MOUTON

THE HAGUE · PARIS

First Printing 1964
Second Printing 1968

Printed in The Netherlands

TABLE OF CONTENTS

INTRODUCTION

Certain basic notions and problems are discussed in this chapter, along with some suggestions for rewrite operations on grammatical formulae.

THE NOTION OF GRAMMAR

How is grammar related to other aspects of linguistic structure? Until recently American structural linguistics has assumed a model of language in which phonemes built into morphemes which in turn built into syntactic units. As a result, phonology, morphology, and syntax were regarded as successively higher layers of structure. Generative grammar has turned this model upside down and ordered it rule-wise with a cover symbol for sentence as the first rule and phonological rules for transcription into terminal sentences as the last section of rules. However novel may be certain aspects of generative grammar, it has not challenged the model in any essential way.[1]

The present procedures are based on a more radical departure from former American structuralism than that found in generative grammar. It is here assumed that language is structured in three semiautonomous but interlocking modes, phonology, grammar, and lexicon (Pike's trimodalism). Phonology is not taken up into morphology which is in turn taken up into syntax. Conversely,

[1] It may be objected that we are confusing representation with structure. Transform grammar claims, however, to provide insight into the nature of language by giving formal expression to our deepest intuitions about language. Transform grammar cannot brush off criticism with the reply that certain devices and ways of talking are merely representational symbols while claiming at the same time that these symbols give adequate expression to linguistic reality.

syntactic and morphological units can not directly be rewritten into component phonological units without omitting some of the relevant aspects of phonology. Although morphemes, words, and sentences do have a phonological structure, phonemes as such are elements in the lowest level of phonological construction (often the syllable), which is in turn relevant to the next ascending level of phonological construction (often the stress group or juncture group), and so on. Similarly, morphemes are elements in the lowest level of grammatical construction (often the word), which is in turn relevant to the next ascending level of grammatical construction (often the phrase), and so on. Morphemes do not necessarily coincide with syllables, nor phonological words (stress groups or juncture groups) with grammatical words. Nor must phonological phrases coincide with grammatical phrases, nor phonological sentences with grammatical sentences. A certain amount of congruence between phonological and grammatical constructions may be expected along with a certain inevitable incongruence. We may with equal propriety describe the grammatical structure of phonological strings and the phonological structure of grammatical strings.

Lexicon is a third mode of linguistic structuring. It is sufficiently separate from grammar that the description of the interplay of item and context, of idiom formation, and of lexical strings (set up by techniques similar to those employed by Harris in his *Discourse Analysis*) is a study within itself.[2] To describe a language exhaustively (a task as yet seriously attempted by no one), three volumes are needed: a phonological statement, a grammatical statement, and a highly sophisticated dictionary. Attempts to incorporate the lexicon directly into the grammar will lead only to the oversimplification of the former or to the endless atomization of the latter.[3]

[2] This is discussed in detail in a paper of mine: "Prolegomena to Lexical Structure", *Linguistics*, 5 (1964), pp. 5-24.

[3] Compare Lees, *Grammar of English Nominalizations*, *IJAL* 26, no. 3, Part II (1960), pp. 20-3. Under "Lexicon", Lees lists 47 word classes presented as follows: Aa mysterious, nice, obvious, understandable ... Ad green, long, old, sad, wise. ... In every case the use of suspension points indicates that the list is exemplary and suggestive. Obviously, a partial listing of this sort will not allow one to generate all possible sentences. For the latter an exhaustive cross reference dictionary would be necessary. In bulk such a work would be many

Similarly, attempts to combine grammar and phonology in one complex set of rules[4] must inevitably result in continued neglect of such units as the syllable and stress group – in spite of the fact that the former is so basic to linguistic structure that most writing systems devised in the ancient Near East were syllabaries.

These procedures develop, then, a method for grammatical analysis as distinguished from both phonological and lexical analysis. Grammatical analysis leads to formulae, statements, and operations which can generate the grammatical patterns of novel utterances beyond the scope of one's corpus. But, until joined to a full set of phonological rules (not a truncated set) and to a complete cross reference dictionary, the grammatical specifications cannot generate actual utterances. This is, however, not a deficiency rooted in the particular sort of grammatical analysis here presented. No grammar, whatever its profession of being generative, that does not generate satisfactory phonological strings (syllables, stress groups, pause groups, and others) with all the fullness of the living language and that is based on anything short of an unrestricted lexicon, can generate in satisfactory and unrestricted fashion *all* the utterances of a language.[5]

---

times greater than the grammatical rules contained in Lees' volume. Only with great awkwardness could it be incorporated into such a volume.

[4] Phonological rules can with no great difficulty be incorporated into a grammar whenever those rules cover phonological groupings congruent with the grammar (and with the restricted lexicon contained within it). But phonological groupings askew with the grammar and/or lexicon would be difficult to handle in a generative grammar as at present conceived. While Stockwell is to be commended for his pioneer work in attempting to incorporate intonation into generative grammars ("The Place of Intonation in a Generative Grammar of English", *Language* 36.360-7, 1960). his article implicitly assumes that the unit relative to the intonation contour (or a concatenated sequence of such contours) is grammatically a sentence as well. Thus, his first rule is S → Nuc. + IP (intonation pattern), while his second rule is Nuc → NP + VP (Chomsky's S → NP + VP). I do not believe this to be so. Rather, two or more grammatically independent sentences may be run together into one phonological sentence with unifying intonation, as shown in the English example in 13.1.(1) and the footnote found there.

[5] Of course a grammar may be constructed which contains a restricted but representative cross section of the lexicon. A properly recursive grammar (allowing for indefinite nesting of a construction type within the same or different

THE NOTION OF ANALYSIS

Our approach is frankly analytic and taxonomic. Neither "analysis" nor "taxonomy" are words lacking in scholarly or scientific status. Statements about languages are inevitably based on an examination of a corpus of some sort – whether a recorded and transcribed corpus or a corpus assembled by the speaker-analyst who describes whatever comes to his mind (and who may curiously fail to call to mind expressions used daily by himself and others). As a protest against certain sterilities in former American structuralism, generative grammar reminds us that the grammatical patterns which we describe must be capable of extrapolation beyond the corpus. Well and good. But generative grammar itself is by no means uninterested in linguistic analysis.[6] Rather the thrust of generative grammar is that attention to tranforms provides at once both a better analysis and a more succinct presentation.

Taxonomic sciences continue to flourish, nor do their practitioners regard "taxonomy" as a bad word. For example, although entomologists have catalogued over 600,000 species of insects, they continue to seek out, catalogue, and study new species in that they suspect that only a small fraction of the world's insects have so far been described. With but a small proportion of the world's 4000 or so languages under formal study, linguists may be in no better a position than entomologists – if, indeed, our position is even as favorable. Surely a project demanding attention is the broadening of the frontiers of human knowledge by the study of an adequate

---

construction types) of this sort can generate an infinite corpus of utterances that are lexically and grammatically satisfying. But it can by no means generate every possible utterance. Rather, it will generate a set of utterances having the property of conformity to the representative but limited lexicon. The reader of even the most carefully constructed generative grammar can formulate utterances with other lexical properties only by resort to intuitively felt patterns of analogy and extrapolation – exactly as in traditional grammars. Furthermore, utterances generated by recursive grammars with restrictive lexicons may fail to be phonologically authentic. Thus, the sentences that are generated are not natural sentences of the language as such but close analogues of such sentences.
[6] In Lees' article "A Multiply Ambiguous Adjectival Construction in English" (*Language* 36.207-21, 1960) he devotes more than a third of the article to a section called "Analysis".

cross-section of the world's languages, many of which are spoken by aboriginal groups only a generation or two from extinction as linguistic entities. However developed may be the *a priori* notion of the nature of language (and a good theory is imperative), empirical investigation of the actual facts of linguistic structure is needed to validate, correct, and round out that notion.

To what degree, then, is linguistics a taxonomic science? This is surely a question to which this generation of linguists should give considerable attention. But this question can not even be entertained by those who have already decided that taxonomy has no place in linguistics. Nevertheless, it seems obvious that the various units and relations of a language can be laid out, classified, and labelled in a manner not unlike the cataloguing of flora and fauna with labelled identification of their functioning parts. On the other hand, generative grammar has conclusively demonstrated that a considerable part of the structure of a language may be described step-wise in formal rules similar to those of a mathematical system. Generative grammar has further shown that such formal rules make explicit and testable notions that otherwise are likely to be ill-defined and unassailable. Need taxonomy and generation be opposed as logically irreconcilable viewpoints? Or is this oppostion one more of those unnecessary and time-consuming pseudo-conflicts with which the history of human thought is strewn? If all grammars worthy of the name are in some sense generative and if even current writings in generative grammar can not escape some analysis, identification, and labelling, then the generation-versus-taxonomy opposition is one with which we should rightly have little patience.

THE NATURE OF PROCEDURE

The procedures here outlined are guess-and-check procedures. Obviously, they are neither mechanically effective nor complete. They need be neither to be useful. Furthermore, the procedures need not be applied in the order here presented, but can be applied at the discretion of the analyst. He may, e.g., want to apply procedures of chapter III (word level procedures) before those of chapter I (clause level procedures). Or, it may prove feasible to work for a time on procedure 2 (clause types), then skip over to procedure 3 (clause level tagmemes), and return later to finish up procedure 2.

In using these procedures we assume the following situation: An analyst approaches a language which either he already knows in some practical way or with which he sets about to familiarize himself – preferably in a language learning situation. The analyst's background is the sum total of his practical knowledge of other languages, his previous analytical experience, and what he has learned from the linguistic research of other people. With this knowledge of the language to be analyzed and with this background knowledge, he makes certain guesses about the grammatical structure of the language. He then submits these guesses to a series of systematic checks in which he confirms, disproves, or modifies his original guesses – and makes a few better guesses en route. This systematic evaluation is based on a theory of the structure of language, and the theory itself (while containing elements of creative thinking) is based on empirical study.

Can only the check be codified then, but not the guess? Obviously, there is an imaginative element in the guess. Nevertheless, as empirical investigation of the grammars of the world's languages moves forward, the range and variety of grammatical constructions will be increasingly well known. At present, enough is known about sound systems of the world's languages that systematic phonetics is now a reality.[7] In this same fashion the time will come when the etics of grammar will be similarly capable of formulation. This formulation will then be available to guide the beginning guesses of the student of a previously unanalyzed language.

PROCEDURE AND THEORY

Any useful procedures must be based on an adequate theory of the

[7]   Cf. Pike's codification (*Phonetics*, Ann Arbor, 1943) and Hockett's (*Manual of Phonology*, Baltimore, 1955).

nature of language. It follows, then, that the very attempt to elaborate procedures may help refine a linguistic theory, while attempts
to apply procedure in a field situation can lead to refinements in
both procedure and theory. It is not unreasonable to insist that any
linguistic theory worthy of the name be expected to give enough
insight into the nature of language to afford practical suggestions as
to what we may find in the grammar of a previously unstudied language. A codification of such suggestions yields discovery procedure.

The theory of language on which these procedures are based has
been developed and expounded by Pike in his *Language in Relation
to a Unified Theory of the Structure of Human Behavior*. This theory
assumes that whatever may be the difficulties in studying and evaluating human behavior in relation to language, behavior is nevertheless more objective and observable than intuition or introspec-
tion. We can observe behavior; we can only affirm intuition.

Central to human behavior is PATTERNING. A noted encephalo-
graphist has written astutely about patterning: "The first significant
attribute of a pattern is that you can remember it and compare it
with another pattern. This is what distinguishes it from random
events or chaos. For the notion of random ... implies that disorder
is beyond comparison; you cannot remember chaos or compare one
chaos with another chaos; there is no plural of the word. Pattern is
a quality of familiar things and familiar things are comparable. It
is much nearer the truth to say that man abhors chaos than to say
that nature abhors a vacuum. ... Broadly speaking one may say
that the sciences derive from pattern-seeking, the arts from pattern-
making, though there in a much more intimate relation between the
seeking and making of patterns than this would suggest."[8]

Granted the centrality of patterning in human behavior it follows
that we should require that a linguistic theory give centrality to
linguistic patterns. In measuring the fit of a theory with the empirical
facts of individual languages we should require that a theory lead to
a description in which patterns are thrown into bold relief. Or, in
terms of evaluating two grammars of the same language, one im-

[8] W. Grey Walter, *The Living Brain*, p. 69 (New York, 1953).

portant criterion of evaluation is that we recognize as superior the grammar which sets forth the patterns of a language in the more straightforward and direct manner. It may be questioned whether linguistic patterns presented obliquely via a set of rewrite rules meet this requirement. The reader of such a set of rules must to some degree deduce patterns from rules; in no one rule is a pattern assembled in summary form. Furthermore, in that the main concern of a compiler of such rules is to frame and order his rules so as to produce terminal sentences as parsimoniously as possible (hence the use of transform rules to supplement rewrite rules), it is not a focal concern that rules at various stages reflect intermediate linguistic patterns. Indeed, with increasing animus the transform school of grammar is rejecting the very concept of linguistic units (e.g. morpheme and phoneme) in their activistic preoccupation with rules.[9]

The brand of grammar here exemplified (tagmemics) attempts to present linguistic patterns in straightforward and summary fashion – although elaboration of a pattern is necessarily step-wise and detailed. Such patterns when carefully described for one language may be compared and contrasted with patterns described for another language. That tagmemics labels linguistic patterns in some fashion is here an advantage; it is difficult to compare things that do not bear names. Patterns thus described and labelled conform to "the first significant attribute of a pattern" (comparability) mentioned in the paragraph quoted above.

Aside from this general argument in favor of linguistic patterns, we argue that CLOSURE and CHOICE, observed in people's use of language, also point to the reality of linguistic patterning. The speaker acts as if he were using units which start and stop. He backtracks and corrects himself if proper closure is not given. He hesitates at certain points as if he were confronted with a choice of item or construction. After partially or wholly articulating one item or construction he may backtrack and correct himself by choosing another item or construction. The hearer likewise demands closure of units and has opinions about choices – as is often evident

[9] Cf. Chomsky, "The Logical Basis of Linguistic Theory", to appear in the *Proceedings of the Ninth International Congress of Linguists*.

by his responses. Speaker and hearer alike seem to be doing something more direct than applying a complicated series of rules to speech; rather they seem to be referring to an inventory of patterns.

Pattern and pattern point therefore are properly primitives of linguistic structure. The particular linguistic theory here followed terms the former SYNTAGMEME (construction)[10] and the latter TAGMEME (element of a construction). The two concepts are correlative. Syntagmemes cannot exist without component elements, i.e. tagmemes. On the other hand, tagmemes exist only by virtue of placement in one or more syntagmemes. As a pattern point the tagmeme involves more than the mere labelling of a node in a tree.[11] In the first place, decisions forced by tagmemic analysis determine whether or not there is to be a node at all, and how many branches the node is to have (e.g. 3.1.-3.9.). A tagmeme is posited only when it can be functionally justified. Furthermore, identification and labelling of tagmemes makes explicit and focal functions which would otherwise be only implicit and peripheral. The tagmeme is a functional point (not necessarily a point in fixed linear sequence) at which a set of

[10]   In my article "String Constituent Analysis" I use HYPERTAGMEME rather than SYNTAGMEME. While the latter term seems to be preferable to the former, the change in terminology reflects no change in underlying theory.

[11]   The function-set correlation embodied in the tagmeme does not necessitate extra nodes in a tree; it results merely in a more precise identification of the node. Thus, a rewrite grammar may contain such a rule as:

S → noun phrase, verb phrase

This rule may be alternatively phrased:

Cl → S:noun phrase, P:verb phrase.

However, tagmemics would not be content with a rule stated in this form. It would want precise identification of the clause type involved, and of the types of noun phrases and verb phrases which can manifest subject and predicate respectively. In particular, "verb phrase" as used in transform grammars (including all sorts of complements and objects as well as modifiers of time, place, and manner) seems much too broad to be useful.

It is essential that a theory and its applications be judged against the background of its own basic assumptions not against a background of alien assumptions. Otherwise, we might better discuss the basic assumptions themselves. Tagmemics assumes the dynamic unity of function and set as mutually correlative concepts; it must therefore be permitted to construct trees in accordance with this assumption. Such trees will contain nodes that consist of function-sets. It is useless to argue that on differing assumptions two nodes would be necessary for a function-set rather than one.

items and/or sequences occur. So intimate is the correlativity of function and set that each is mutually dependent on the other; the function cannot exist apart from the set nor has the set significance apart from the function. Thus the tagmeme concept restores function to its rightful place in grammar.

The various patterns and pattern points of a language are not a loose inventory available to the speaker but comprise a system. How may relations among patterns be shown? Generative grammar has brought forcibly and commendably to our attention the usefulness of grammatical transforms as one means of expressing relations between sentences. Grammatical matrix theory (not to be confused with matrix algebra) as being currently developed by Pike[12] offers a way of showing relations between constructions in general (not merely between sentences) by conceptualizing them as charted together in various dimensions. The two ways of showing relations are not immiscible; both are incorporated to some degree in these procedures.

The most obvious way in which constructions on different levels of structure (not levels of representation) are related within a language is by virtue of grammatical hierarchy. Immediate constituent analysis yielded *ad hoc* hierarchies specialized overmuch in terms of particular sentences. Immediate constituent analysis failed, therefore, to uncover hierarchically arranged patterns of maximum relevance and comparability. It tended rather to endless fragmentation in which the picture was obscured by overstructuring at some points. The system of dichotomous binary cutting – which was the normal way of operation in this analysis – had no way of distinguishing comparatively relevant from comparatively irrelevant cuts.[13] Tagmemics, in that it is functionally oriented, clears up this confusion; it assumes that every language has a grammatical hierarchy discoverable within the framework of that language and applicable to the language as a whole. Tagmemics thus carefully

---

[12]   Pike, "Dimensions of Grammatical Structure", *Language* 38.221-44 (1962).
[13]   For criticism of immediate constituent analysis and presentation of systemic grammatical hierarchy, see Longacre, "String Constituent Analysis", *Language* 36.63-88 (1960), and Zvelebil "How to Handle the Structure of Tamil", *Archiv Orientální* 30.116-42 (1962).

distinguishes emic levels from mere layering tendencies and from multiple nesting of type within type on the same level. One frequently found hierarchical arrangement consists of the following five levels (plus further possible levels such as paragraph and discourse): stem, word, phrase, clause, and sentence.[14] Typically, syntagmemes of one structural level manifest tagmemes of the next higher level; e.g., words manifest phrase level tagmemes. But a syntagmeme may manifest a tagmeme of another syntagmeme on the same level; e.g., one phrase may occur imbedded within another phrase. As a variant of the latter one syntagmeme may nest recursively within the same syntagmeme to an infinite number of layers. Finally, on occasion, a syntagmeme of a higher level may manifest a tagmeme of a lower level; e.g. a subordinate clause may occur within a phrase.

Systematic hierarchy of this sort is an important feature of language. It is required of a linguistic theory that it not obscure grammatical hierarchy nor relations within that hierarchy.

If patterns are comparable (and comparing patterns seems to be a natural and wholesome human activity), then it follows that we need criteria to distinguish one pattern from another. Similarly, we need criteria for distinguishing the structurally significant points within a given pattern. Much of these procedures consists in setting forth these two sorts of criteria in detail. While the criteria for

[14] Total accountability for all linguistic data in the corpus is not required as a defining property of a level of structure. While all the data of the corpus are divisible into roots and into sentences without residue on either level, all the data are not necessarily accounted for on intermediate levels. The lowest level, that of roots, is not a level of construction as such but rather of building blocks entering into constructions. It follows, therefore, that the corpus is divisible without residue into roots. Sentences are characterized by a degree of closure (but not necessarily phonological juncture, cf. 13.1) not characteristic of lower levels. We consider to be sentences certain constructions consisting of elliptical clauses and of phrases. For this reason the data of a corpus usually turn out to be wholly divisible into sentences without residue. But there seems to be no good reason for considering that a sentence consisting of a phrase necessarily has the structure of a clause as well. To do so would only obscure the defining properties of the clause. Similarly, a language may contain low-level structures (e.g., pronouns) which never expand into phrases but enter directly into the structure of clauses. Little would be gained by calling such unexpandable items phrases. Nor is much gained by calling them words. Rather, they are roots.

separating pattern points (tagmemes) are relatively straightforward, the criteria for separating the patterns themselves (syntagmemes) are of necessity more complicated. Thus, any clear difference – including distinctions in linear ordering – can establish a contrast between two tagmemes. But we require more then this to distinguish two syntagmemes: FOR TWO PATTERNS (SYNTAGMEMES) TO BE IN CONTRAST THEY MUST HAVE MORE THAN ONE STRUCTURAL DIFFERENCE BETWEEN THEM; AT LEAST ONE OF THESE DIFFERENCES MUST INVOLVE THE NUCLEI OF THE SYNTAGMEMES. In practice this amounts to insistence on a two-fold minimal difference at least one of which involves the nuclei.

To show two patterns to be in contrast we need evidence that they are in contrast qua patterns. Consider the plight of the analyst confronted with a language where a single verb may be inflected to become 5000 different forms. Many of these forms are very similar to each other; the distinctions involved seem to affect only certain local points within the stem-affix string. Other forms seem to be quite distinct; we suspect that not only are pattern points affected but that the patterns themselves differ. What sort of minimal contrast separates patterns from each other? One difference is insufficient in that it may be relevant to but one point in the patterns being contrasted and may not indicate that the patterns themselves are in contrast. If the patterns are in contrast they should differ at more than one point. Furthermore, a difference between patterns should surely affect the nuclei of the patterns, not merely their peripheries. Patterns can scarcely be considered to contrast if they do not differ in their most essential and characteristic parts.

Criteria for distinguishing nuclei from peripheries are given under clause level procedures (2.1.) and phrase level procedures (6.1.). In that nuclear and obligatory tagmemes are often equivalent on the word and sentence levels these sections of the procedures (chapters III and IV) are set up in terms of obligatory versus optional tagmemes. This modification is in the interest of procedural feasibility; it in no way abrogates our stand that for two syntagmemes to be in contrast they must differ in their nuclei.[15]

[15] Introduction of the nuclear-peripheral distinction (Pickett, 1960) provides a

Keeping in mind the very important qualification that the two-fold minimal contrast must affect the nuclei, countable structural differences between two syntagmemes would seem to be such features as (a) differing linear orderings; (b) differing number of tagmemes; (c) differing syntagmemes manifesting similar but distinct tagmemes; (d) differing emic classes manifesting similar but distinct tagmemes; (e) differing transform potential (or differing derivations via transform).

An emic class is either a small closed function set (an order of affixes or a group of function particles of the sort posited in Fries' *Structure of English*), or a subdivision of a large and open hyperclass (e.g., a subdivision including some but not all verbs). In the latter case the words grouped as an emic class should be relevant to at least two spots in the grammar – with one spot not transformationally related to the other. In this fashion one can avoid counting co-occurrence groupings as grammatically significant. Lexical co-occurrence restrictions characterize the manifestations of most constructions of any length and complexity. Given a construction, not any lexeme manifesting one of its tagmemes can co-occur with any lexeme manifesting another of its tagmemes; cartesian multiplication is not uniformly possible. Care must be taken here lest significant grammatical patterns be obscured by the proliferation of types based on which lexemes manifesting X can occur with lexemes manifesting Y (versus Q with R, Z with W, etc.). One thing is certain: if such lexical co-occurrences are stated exhaustively today, they will change with the novel utterance spoken tomorrow. Furthermore, the analyst who sets himself to trace all such co-occurrence phenomena launches himself on a course which has no necessary stopping point short of that imposed by his own fatigue.

The criterion for minimal contrast between syntagmemes rules

---

needed tertium quid not found in the simple dichotomy obligatory versus optional. Especially on the clause and phrase levels (where procedures are explicitly set up in terms of nucleus versus periphery) we often encounter optional tagmemes of considerable relevance in defining syntagmemes. Such tagmemes can now be considered to be nuclear although optional. We thus evolve a trichotomous classification: (1) Nuclear and obligatory, (2) Nuclear and optional, (3) Peripheral (and optional).

out, therefore, setting up a contrast on such a basis as: There is a syntagmeme AB with two component tagmemes A and B. We may subdivide the items manifesting A into A′ and A″, and may likewise subdivide the items manifesting B into B′ and B″. A′ co-occurs with B′, while A″ co-occurs with B″. The subdivisions of the manifestations of A and B constitute lists which are of relevance only here and in one other construction which is a transform of this one. In this case we do not consider that the subdivisions constitute emic classes nor that A′B′ is a separate syntagmeme from A″B″. Rather we set up A′B′ and A″B″ as co-occurrence (lexically determined) variants of the one syntagmeme AB.[16] Our primary interest in the grammar is the syntagmemes and their component tagmemes along with interrelations of syntagmemes. We trace out as many co-occurrence variants as we have time and energy. Ultimately, the task of tracing out collocational compatibilities is that of the lexicographer.

Contrasting external distribution of two constructions is also ruled out as a structural difference countable in separating syntagmemes. The Latin phrase *puella bona* 'good girl' with nominative case ending is not considered to be different in phrase type from *puellae bonae* with genitive-dative case ending, nor from *puellam bonam* with accusative case ending. An argument could be made for separating these phrases on the grounds that (1) they have one internal structural difference, viz. choice of case ending; and (2) they differ in distribution within clause and phrase structures. But is such a separation desirable? A Latin noun has the following structure: +ns +cn (ns = noun stem of a given gender, cn = case-number ending of but one gender[17]). An adjective has the structure: +as +cng (as = adjective stem, cng = case-number-gender

---

[16] For a very fine discussion of etic variants of syntagmemes see Pike, "Dimensions of Grammatical Structure", pp. 235-43.

[17] The inherent gender of a stem takes precedence over the apparent gender of the ending whenever the two conflict as in *nauta* 'sailor" which is modified by *bonus* 'good'. For this and other reasons (considerations of hierarchical structurings) it would seem best to analyze noun endings occurring in a noun phrase as occurring several times rather than as constituting one discontinuous morpheme which occurs with the whole phrase (as in Harris, "Discontinuous Morphemes", *Language*, 21. 121-7).

endings running through three genders). A given noun stem occurs
with ten case-number endings. An adjective stem occurs with
thirty case-number-gender endings. A noun or adjective has the
same internal two-tagmeme structure regardless of which ending is
selected for it. Choice of a particular ending is not relevant as such
to the structure of nouns and adjectives. Nor is choice of one
ending versus another relevant as such to the structure of noun
phrases – aside from the fact that the agreement within the phrase
binds it together as a structural entity overtly marked. Here, however, it is the fact of agreement that is important rather than the
occurrence of a given case, number, and gender. At all events,
puella bears the same relation to *bona* that *puellam* does to *bonam*.
It is only when a phrase is imbedded in another phrase (*pecunia
puellae bonae* 'the money of the good girl'), or on the clause level
(*puellam bonam amat* 'he loves the good girl') that choice of particular endings becomes relevant. On the phrase level itself nothing
but gratuitous complexity is gained from separating *puellae bonae*
and *puellam bonam* as separate phrase types (syntagmemes). Such a
separation automatically multiplies all noun phrase types in Latin
by ten and obscures structural distinctions proper to the phrase
level (e.g., possessive phrase versus attributive phrase) by merging
them with distinctions from other levels (subject versus object versus
indirect object, etc.).

We object, therefore, to considering external distribution of a
syntagmeme to be a countable contrastive feature[18] on the following
scores: (1) It tends to obscure structural distinctions proper to one
level by overlaying them with distinctions proper to another level.
(2) By so doing, it tends to jeopardize the very concept of structural
levels and grammatical hierarchy. (3) External distribution of a
construction only approximately correlates with its internal structure. It is as useless to attempt to force congruence of internal struc-

---

[18] For an application of the two-fold structural contrast in which external
distribution of a syntagmeme is considered to be relevant, see Pike. "Dimensions of Grammatical Structure", p. 232. Pike believes that the dual criterion
can not be applied in some cases without direct consideration of semantics.
Pike, furthermore, does not insist that the dual structural contrast affect the
nucleus of a syntagmeme.

ture and external distribution as it is to attempt to force congruence of grammatical and phonological boundaries. Thus, by distinguishing internal structure and external distribution – and not merging the two as identifying-contrastive features of syntagmemes – we are less embarrassed on encountering exocentric constructions (which have an external distribution not expected on the basis of their internal structure). (4) External distribution of a syntagmeme may naturally be described in terms of the (usually higher level) tagmemes which that syntagmeme manifests; it need not be a contrastive feature of the syntagmeme itself.[19]

The proper role of external distribution relative to contrast among syntagmemes may be summarized as follows: (1) Syntagmemes are set up as types differing by virtue of contrasting internal structures. (2) Distinct classes of syntagmemes have DISTINCT distributions, e.g. verb phrases versus noun phrases, or dependent versus independent clauses. (3) Within a class of syntagmemes, it is frequently found that contrasting syntagmemes have SIMILAR or IDENTICAL distributions. Thus, several contrasting verb phrases may manifest predicate in the same clause type, several types of noun phrase may manifest subject or object, and several clause types may occur as main clause in the same sentence pattern. If external distribution is to be counted at all as relevant to syntagmemic contrast, it would seem that the similar or identical distributions here mentioned are more relevant than the distinct distributions of (2). (4) Setting up of classes of syntagmemes is logically subsequent to the setting up of the syntagmemes themselves. It follows, therefore, that an *a priori* scheme of classes should not be allowed to dictate the number of syntagmemes that are posited. To do so, is to forsake the empirical approach to grammar. (5) On occasion, however, two similar sequences – not adequately contrastive in internal structure – may be considered to be separate because they belong to different classes

---

[19]   Notice, however, that emic classes are countable as a distinguishing feature of syntagmemes. Emic classes are set up in reference to total distribution of a class in the structure of a language. This, therefore, involves consideration of external distribution. To this degree consideration of external distribution enters indirectly into the analysis of contrasting construction types. But to bring it in directly is to court confusion.

(cf. 2.7.) which are otherwise separable (in that they are constituted by sequences adequately contrasting in internal structure).[20]

MEANING

What is the proper place of meaning in deciding whether or not two patterns are in contrast? Obviously, meaning lurks in the background everywhere. The background of meaning would seem to be essential to the analysis. No one has yet written a grammar of a dead language available only in undeciphered inscriptions. On the other hand, it seems best that meaning nowhere come into the foreground. We assume with Pike that the units we handle are form-meaning composites. Nevertheless, it seems necessary to insist that it is the formal side of the composite which is amenable to initial systemic analysis. We work with formal correlates of meaning. For example, from what we know of meaning, we may suspect that two given constructions contrast with each other. Nevertheless, we never pronounce them to be in contrast until formal contrasts are encountered. The contrasts need not be formal in any narrow, restrictive sense of the word – they may, for example, include difference in transform potential – nevertheless, formal contrasts must be

[20]   There is marked parallelism to phonology here: (1) Most phonemes are phonetically dissimilar and *prima facie* contrastive. Trouble in phonemic analysis typically arises from a relatively small number of the phones encountered. (2) Distinct classes of phonemes (e.g. consonant versus vowel) have distinct distributions. (3) Within a class of phonemes, it is found that contrastive phonemes have similar or identical distributions (English b and p in bit versus pit); indeed the basic postulates of phonemic contrast require something of this sort. (4) Setting up of classes of phonemes should be specific to a given language. Thus, even though vowel and consonant may prove to be cultural universals (the question is not, however, closed) other phoneme classes, e.g. semivowels, tones and laryngeals may be relevant as well. (5) On occasion, however, two similar phones, say i and į may be separated on the grounds that they belong to separate classes (vowel and consonant) which are otherwise contrastive and relevant.

In writing these paragraphs on external distribution I have profited from discussions with Sarah Gudschinsky – especially in regard to the possible importance of similar or identical external distributions in establishing syntagmemic contrast. In the course of our protracted argument over the relevance of differing external distributions both Pike and I have failed to raise this question now raised by Gudschinsky.

found. It is required, therefore, of writers of tagmemic grammars
and grammatical sketches, that they present clearly the formal features which justify an alleged contrast.

SYMBOLS AND REWRITE OPERATIONS

Any consistent use of symbols is inherently mathematical. It may
be that symbols and operations worked out on the terrain of linguistics will prove more satisfactory than unacculturated symbols
brought over uncritically from mathematics proper. A system of
symbols with uniform values should be employed in a grammar.
Furthermore, symbols must be adequately explained if the reader is
to follow the exposition. Both tagmemic and transform grammars
employ extensive symbolism which is not always made intelligible to
the reader. Writers of either sort of grammar should exercise more
care in this regard in future publications.

Tagmemic formulae give map-like summaries of constructions.
Thus, there is a Trique noun phrase type with the following formula:

$$\pm i \pm q + H \pm A \pm d$$

(where i = identifier, q = quantifier, H = head, A = attribute,
and d = deictic). Two devices in this formula show it is not an
analysis of any particular Trique noun phrase but is rather a summary of all possible phrases built on this pattern: (1) The use of the
sign $\pm$ indicates optional presence of a tagmeme. This can not be
an analysis of any particular Trique noun phrase in that a given element must be either present or absent in a given phrase. (2) Each
(letter) symbol indicates a functional point at which a set of manifesting items and/or sequences occurs. In a given phrase but one
member of a manifesting set occurs at a given functional point.

Indication of the set of items occurring at a functional point is
given in one of two ways in tagmemic grammars. A dual function-
set symbolism can indicate the set in the summary formula itself as
follows (the colon means "manifested by"):

$$\pm i: ne^3 h \text{ 'the'} \pm q: \text{num} + H: \text{Nn} \pm A: \text{Ad/Nn} \pm d: \text{dc}$$

(num = numeral, Nn = noun, Ad = adjective, and dc = deictics, nq^3h 'this', mq^3h 'that', and dq^3h 'a certain one'). This dual symbolism has the advantage of putting maximum information into the formula. Furthermore, it forcibly emphasizes the unity of function-set in the tagmeme. It has the disadvantage that, granted intricate substitution possibilities (occurrence of imbedded phrase within phrase, or of certain word classes, phrase types, and subordinate clauses all as manifestations of the same tagmeme) the whole formula becomes involved and unwieldy. A tagmemic grammar may, however, employ another device, i.e. use of unitary symbols for patterns points (tagmemes) with indication of the manifesting sets deferred to subsequent rules. By so doing the map-like structure of a tagmemic formula is retained but less information is put on the map – which must now be taken in conjunction with a set of rules immediately following.

Once constructed, such a formula (or formula with immediately following rules) may be operated on in various ways. These operations may be carried out exhaustively so as to produce all possible grammatical variants of the patterns thus summarized. Or the operations may be carried out so as to trace out from point to point through the grammar the path towards a particular terminal sentence. Production of the actual terminal sentence is dependent, however, on supply of information from cross-referenced studies in phonology and lexicon. If one is content with something less than a complete phonology and with a restricted lexicon (such as characterize transform grammars), terminal sentences may be produced by incorporation of this truncated phonology and lexicon into the grammar.

$\mathcal{R}$ is an operation whereby a particular READING of a formula is obtained as follows: (1) All symbols following plus signs are retained. (2) A given $\pm$ sign is read as either plus or minus; the symbol following it is retained only if it has been read as plus. (3) Superscript ^{2} permits us to read a symbol either once or twice in a given reading. Superscript ^{n} permits us to read a symbol as many times as desired in a given reading.[21] (4) The signs and superscripts

[21] Use of superscript ^{n} in tagmemic formulae is one manner in which such

are removed; the reading of a formula contains only symbols for tagmemes.

$\mathcal{R}$ may be carried out until all possible readings of a formula are exhausted (such exhaustive reading of a formula provides a valuable procedural check on its validity). A tagmemic formula that has no sign but $+$ and no superscripts has but one possible reading. We express this by attaching a subscript $_1$ to $\mathcal{R}$: $\mathcal{R}_1$. Otherwise, the value of subscript of $\mathcal{R}$ is equal to the number of possible readings of a formula.[22]

The formula for a Trique intransitive clause is: $+P_1 +S \pm L^2 \pm T^2$ (P_1 = intransitive predicate, S = subject, L = Locational, T = temporal). Operation $\mathcal{R}$ is exhaustively carried out on this formula as follows (with P_1 simplified notationally to P): $\mathcal{R}(+P +S \pm L^2 \pm T^2)$ = PS, PSL, PST, PSLT, PSLL, PSTT, PSLLT, PSLTT, PSLLTT. In that there are nine possible readings of this formula, $\mathcal{R}$ has a subscript value of nine: $\mathcal{R}_9$.

formulae allow for the open-ended flexibility which characterizes actual use of language. Such formulae allow for tree structures with an indefinite (and theoretically unlimited) number of branches. Multiple nesting of syntagmeme within syntagmeme as seen in sections 2.6., 2.8., 5.6.(2), 7.0.2., 14.5., and 15.1.(4) of these procedures achieves the same end. In particular note the formulae for coordinate constructions on the phrase level in section 6.2. In view of these features of tagmemic formulae it is pointless for advocates of transform grammar to continue to contend that tagmemics cannot handle such problems as infinite branching, infinite nesting, and coordinate constructions admitting formation of an infinite series.

[22]   Value of subscript of $\mathcal{R}$ may be computed by assigning value 0 to every $+$ sign of the formula, and value 1 to every $\pm$ sign; superscripts are taken at numerical value (unmarked symbols are considered to have a superscript of ^{1}). Letting p stand for the signs of a formula and s for the superscripts, value of subscript of $\mathcal{R}$ may be computed by the following formula:

$$(p_a + s_a) \times (p_b + s_b) \times (p_c + s_c) \ldots = x$$

Applying to the formula for Trique intransitive clause above:

$$(0 + 1) \times (0 + 1) \times (1 + 2) \times (1 + 2) = 9.$$

A tagmemic formula with a tagmeme marked with superscript ^{n} has an infinite value for the subscript of $\mathcal{R}$, i.e. it has a (theoretically) unlimited number of readings. Operation $\mathcal{R}$ can be carried out on such a formula to produce any particular reading that is desired. $\mathcal{R}$ may not, however, be exhaustively carried out. A grammar should point out which readings are more probable (which are most frequently found in conversation or text). In general the longer and more complicated a reading is, the less probable is its actualization in a terminal sentence.

$\mathscr{P}$ is an operation on a particular reading whereby the symbols are taken in an order not necessarily that in which they occur in the reading. $\mathscr{P}$ must be performed, therefore, in accordance with particular rules stating possible orderings of the symbols. Carrying out of $\mathscr{P}$ produces a particular PERMUTATION from a particular reading. For a reading symbolizing a structure with no variation in word order (such as the Trique noun phrase whose formula is given above), subscript of $\mathscr{P}$ has a value of 1; the only permutation possible is an identity permutation. Otherwise, the value of subscript of $\mathscr{P}$ is equal to the number of distinct orderings which are possible.[23] The permutation rules accompanying the Trique intransitive clause are two: (1) One symbol at a time may be moved to the left of P. (2) Contiguous LT may vary to TL, but neither may occur bracketed by a cluster of the other (e.g., TLT and LTLT do not occur). In accordance with these rules we exhaustively carry out $\mathscr{P}$ on the particular reading PSLT as follows: $\mathscr{P}$ (PSLT) = PSLT, SPLT, LPST, TPSL, PSTL, SPLT. For the reading PSLT, $\mathscr{P}$ may be carried out six times and may therefore be given a subscript of this value: $\mathscr{P}_6$. Carrying out of this operation on the other eight readings of the formula gives: $\mathscr{P}$ (PS) = PS, SP. $\mathscr{P}$ (PSL) = PSL, SPL, LPS. $\mathscr{P}$ (PST) = PST, SPT, TPS. $\mathscr{P}$ (PSLL) = PSLL, SPLL, LPSL. $\mathscr{P}$ (PSTT) = PSTT, SPTT, TPST. $\mathscr{P}$ (PSLLT) = PSLLT, SPLLT, LPSLT, TPSLL, LPSTL. $\mathscr{P}$ (PSLTT) = PSLTT, SPLTT, LPSTT, TPSLT, TPSTL. $\mathscr{P}$ (PSLLTT) = PSLLTT, SPLLTT, LPSLTT, TPSLLT. A total of 34 permutations results. The total number of permutations of an original formula is the sum of the values of subscript of $\mathscr{P}$ for each $\mathscr{R}$ of the formula.

$\mathscr{E}$ is an operation on a particular permutation whereby each of its symbols is replaced by the label for or formula of one of its exponents (manifestations).[24] Carrying out of $\mathscr{E}$ produces a parti-

---

[23] The number of permutations possible for a given reading is: x!-y (x = number of symbols in a reading; y = number of permutations not possible because of special rules; the x! is factorial, e.g. if x has the value of 4, then $1 \times 2 \times 3 \times 4$).

[24] EXPONENT as used here must not be confused with superscript. Cf. the use of exponent in Halliday's "Categories of the Theory of Grammar" (*Word* 17. 241-292, 1961) and in McIntosh's "Patterns and Ranges" (*Language* 37.325-337

cular exponential combination. Repeated carrying out of $\mathscr{E}$ gives all possible exponential combinations which can occur for a permutation. For such exhaustive carrying out of this operation on a relatively high level formula, assistance from a computer is all but mandatory. In that either the label for or formula of an exponent may be substituted for a symbol, operation $\mathscr{E}$ may be considered to proceed in two stages: (1) substitution of exponential labels; and (2) substitution of the formula corresponding to the label.[25] In the next paragraph the first sort of substitution is illustrated; in two paragraphs below, the second.

PSLT is a particular (identity) permutation of the reading PSLT of the formula for Trique intransitive clause. Tagmeme P has six exponents, S has eleven, L has six, and T has seven. The six exponents of P are:[26] Ph_{11} (active qualifier main verb phrase of intransitive class), Ph_{21} (incorporated goal verb phrase of intransitive class), $Ph_{3\cdot2}$ (nonactive qualifier main verb phrase, subtype 3), Ph_4 (incorporated complement verb phrase), Ph_5 (metaphorical verb phrase), Ph_{61} (repetitive verb phrase of intransitive class). The eleven exponents of S, subject tagmeme, are exemplified by Ph_{11} (qualifier noun phrase). The six exponents of L, locational tagmeme are exemplified by Ph_{411} (relator-axis phrase of locational class). The seven exponents of T are exemplified by Ph_{31} (ordinal temporal phrase). L and T each have an exponent that consists of a subordinate clause, while S has an exponent that consists of a relative sentence. We now carry out operation $\mathscr{E}$ on the permutation PSLT as follows: $\mathscr{E}$ (PSLT) $= Ph_{11} \, Ph_{11} \, Ph_{411} \, Ph_{31}$.

(1961). I use the term here to refer not only to lexical manifestations of constructions and construction points but also to imbedded grammatical constructions which manifest points in more inclusive constructions. The theory of grammar presented by Halliday is in many respects similar to that presented here.

[25] Such substitution in two stages does not of itself indicate two nodes in the tree of a construction. There is but one node, viz. a grammatical point with this particular construction manifesting it. From this node there is multiple branching as indicated in the formula of the included construction.

[26] Labels here consist of three parts: Ph, which may be read "phrase type"; subscript to indicate precise phrase type (the use of a numeral after the decimal point in a subscript indicates a subtype); and letter subscript following number subscript (to indicate emic class of a construction).

Referring to other sections of the grammar, we now proceed to substitute formulae for labels in the above (parentheses will surround each formula): ($\pm$adv $\pm$Aux $+$Mn $\pm$Md $\pm$r) ($\pm$i $\pm$q $+$H $\pm$A $\pm$d) ($+$R $+$Ax) ($+$U $+$Or). The phrase level tagmemes symbolized above are: adv = adverbial manifested by six particles; Aux = auxiliary manifested by some fourteen auxiliary verbs; Mn = main manifested by any intransitive verb and by a few exocentric constructions: r = repetitive manifested by the particle yu^2 'again'; for i, q, H, A, d see above; R = relator manifested by prepositions; Ax = axis manifested by any noun phrase type; U = unit manifested by a few nouns meaning 'hour', 'day', 'month', 'year', and 'Friday of Lent'; Or = ordinal manifested by numeral plus syntactic up-glide which indicates end of noun phrase.

Exhaustive carrying out of $\mathcal{E}$ for the permutation PSLT should theoretically yield 2772 exponential combinations, viz. the product of $6 \times 11 \times 6 \times 7$. A few special constraints (which must be stated in the grammar) rule out certain exponential combinations. For example, although L has a subordinate clause as one of its exponents, that particular exponent of L cannot be substituted in PSLT. If a subordinate clause were to be an exponent of L in PSLT, then the following exponent of T would be attracted into the subordinate clause from the main clause. The formula for the main clause would then turn out to be PSL rather than PSLT. This constraint reduces the exponents of L relevant to PSLT from six to five and brings the mathematically possible number of exponential combinations down to 2310. Nevertheless, exhaustive carrying out of $\mathcal{E}$ for all 34 permutations deducible from readings of the formula for intransitive clause in Trique should yield somewhere around 200,000 exponential combinations.

Once one has carried out operations $\mathcal{R}$, $\mathcal{P}$, and $\mathcal{E}$ (in both stages) on a tagmemic formula he may further preceed to: (1) Carry out operations $\mathcal{R}$, $\mathcal{P}$, and $\mathcal{E}$ on the formulae left as a result of the second stage of operation $\mathcal{E}$ – thus obtaining readings, permutations, and exponential combinations for each formula in turn. For example, each formula in the string of four formulae given two paragraphs above can be given a particular reading as follows: (adv Aux Mn)

(H A d) (R Ax) (U Or). No permutations of Trique phrase types are possible except the identity permutation. This is equivalent to saying that order of tagmemes is fixed in Trique phrases. Each and every reading of a Trique phrase has $\mathscr{P}$ with a subscript value of 1: $\mathscr{P}_1$. Carrying out of operation $\mathscr{E}$ in the above string of four readings results in substutition of (a) a label for a word structure e.g. W_5 (aspect-mood verbs); or (b) a label for an imbedded phrase structure, e.g. Ph_{11}; or (c) an actual functional morpheme. We carry out this operation on the string of four permutations: (a^5P 'already' $W_{5aux} W_6$) (Noun Adjective dq^3h 'a certain') (ri^3ki^3 'among', 'down in' Ph_{11}) (gwi^3 'day' Ph_{61}). In the above, $Ph_{61} =$ vigesmal numeral phrase. (2) Remove the parentheses in the resultant string. Thus, the above string would now be (omitting translation glosses): a^5P $W_{5aux} W_5$ Noun Adjective dq^3h ri^3ki^3 Ph_{11} gwi^3 Ph_{61}. (3) Carry out operations $\mathscr{R}$, $\mathscr{P}$, and $\mathscr{E}$ on any remaining labels for syntagmemes, such as W_{5aux}, W_5, Ph_{11}, and Ph_{61}. Unless there is further imbedding of phrase type within phrase type, one should now obtain a string where no labels for syntagmemes remain but only functional morphemes and names of word or stem classes. Thus, the string obtained at end of (2) above could become (by choices of particular readings and exponential combinations; permutations again have subscript value of one and may be disregarded): q^5P (asp mood vs') (aspect mood vs') Noun Adjective dq^3h ri^3ki^3 (Noun dq^3h) gwi^3 (sc int). In the above, asp = aspect; vs' = a class of verb stems; sc = score; int = integer. (4) Remove parentheses in the above, but indicate bound forms by hyphens. (5) Resort to a cross reference lexicon in order to substitute specific lexical items for names of word and stem classes. Indications of aspect and mood will be supplied according to particular allomorphs of aspectual and modal morphemes as given in the dictionary. Thus, the string which has gone through several rewrite stages[27] above might come out: a^5P $gq^3Pq^{34}h$ ga^5wi^5P $žu^3we^3$ ga^5ci^5 dq^3h ri^3ki^3 cu^3 dq^3h gwi^3 go^4 gq^5Pq^3h. 'Already went to die the white dog under that box the twenty-fourth day', i.e., 'On the twenty-fourth

[27] For a step-by-step summary of the rewrite operations producing this semi-terminal string, see the appendix of this introduction.

day that white dog had already crawled under the box to die'. (6) Give the lexical string proper phonological structure. Such phonological information, if it is to be complete and adequate, must be given semiautonomous development in a cross reference work on phonology similar to the projected cross reference dictionary. Without supply of this phonological information, the lexical string given under (5) is not, properly speaking, a terminal sentence (of one clause structure) but is rather semiterminal. It has several possible phonological structurings (patterns of stress and rhythm with relative degree of spread of tone intervals). Also, the allophones of various phonemes will vary according to the rate of speed of utterance.

The path of rewrite operations that may be traced through a tagmemic grammar is uni-directional — although it may involve recursive loopings on the same level and back-loopings to a higher level. If a grammar is written proceeding from word structure to sentence structure, then the rewrite path will, as a whole, be one winding from the rear of the grammar thus written towards its front. Rewrite paths winding from front to rear are possible if higher levels of grammatical structure (sentence and clause) are presented before lower levels. Nevertheless, the latter course necessitates extensive forward reference to structures as yet undescribed, while the former course proceeds from described to undescribed structures. But there seems to be no inherent reason why a back winding rewrite path can not be fully as useful as a forward winding one. At any rate, multiple choices confront one at many junctures: in choosing a particular reading, a particular permutation, a particular exponential combination, and finally a particular lexical and phonological structuring. But regardless of the rewrite path that one chooses to follow through a tagmemic grammar, he will end up with the grammatically possible and never with the grammatically impossible — provided the grammar has been carefully constructed.

It should be evident that a set of tagmemic formulae has considerable generative power and that the generation of constructions from such formulae can be made quite explicit. Writers of generative grammars of any school will have to wrestle with lexical and phonological complications which may limit the scope of their grammars. Nevertheless, if any variety of generative grammar can produce semiterminal sentences of correct grammatical patterns within the limits of a restricted lexicon phonemically transcribed, this is no mean accomplishment.

Tagmemic grammars have up to the present time been content to present formulae (accompanied by statements) in nonformalized fashion. Such grammars can (and should) be more explicitly formalized. Rewrite operations of the sort here suggested are implicit in tagmemic grammars but have not been made explicit. Future tagmemic grammars might well employ these operations by (a) stating them in the front of the grammar, (b) carrying them out in illustrative fashion here and there through the grammar, and (c) incorporating sections of rewrite exercises for the reader. In that rewrite operations of the sort here described are applicable to any tagmemic formula in any language anywhere, they achieve a universality not found in specific rewrite rules applicable to but one language. A grammar can employ such rewrite operations without obscuring linguistic patterning in that the fundamental place in such a grammar will still be given to presentation of syntagmeme and tagmeme. Such a grammar should therefore commend itself as both taxonomic and generative.

ACKNOWLEDGMENTS

Besides occasional reference to English, data to illustrate these procedures come from published and unpublished studies of the following languages:

Otomanguean: Chatino (Kitty Pride), Trique (Longacre), Isthmus Zapotec (Pickett)

Mayan: Aguacatec, (McArthur), Ixil (Elliott), Jacaltec (Church), K'ekchi' (Eachus), Tzotzil (Delgaty), Quiché (Fox)

Other American Indian: Amuesha (Wise), Apache (Hoijer), Candoshi (Cox), Cashibo (Shell), Choctaw (data file, Summer Institute of Linguistics, Norman, Okla.), Chontal of Oaxaca (Waterhouse), Potawatomi (Hockett), Seminole (West), Zoque (Engel, Wonderly)

Malayo-Polynesian: Cebuano (Flores), Maranao (McKaughan)

Others: Fore of New Guinea (Scott via Pike), Tairora of New Guinea (Vincent), Hebrew (Longacre), Bengali (Mohiyud-Din)

Many of the above are colleagues of the Summer Institute of Linguistics. Special stimulus for the writing of these procedures was gained from two field workshops held in Guatemala (1958) and in Mexico (1962) under the auspices of this Institute, and from a field methods class at the University of Michigan (1960). Term papers by native speakers of Cebuano, Tagalog, Indonesian, Korean, Japanese, Thai, Urdu, and Bengali further demonstrated the usefulness of the tagmemic approach in languages other than American Indian,[28] and have made a vital contribution to the development of these procedures.

Special acknowledgment is made here to Bruce Moore, Joseph Grimes, Barbara Erickson, Esther Matteson, Carolyn Orr, and Sarah Gudschinsky, for vigorous and helpful criticism of particular sections of this volume; to Lucille Schneider for her careful and critical typing; to McKaughan's Maranao study for the terms single centered, double centered, and noncentered; to Nida and Harris for early stimulus in nontagmemic grammatical analysis; and to Pike to whom I am indebted in too pervasive a fashion for detailed acknowledgment.

APPENDIX: SUMMARY OF REWRITE OPERATIONS ON FORMULA OF TRIQUE INTRANSITIVE CLAUSE

1. Formula of Trique intransitive clause: $+\text{Pi} +\text{S} \pm\text{L}^2 \pm\text{T}^2$ (Pi is simplified to P below).
2. $\mathscr{R} (+\text{P} +\text{S} \pm\text{L}^2 \pm\text{T}^2) = \text{PSLT}$.
3. $\mathscr{P} (\text{PSLT}) = \text{PSLT}$ (identity permutation).
4. $\mathscr{E} (\text{PSLT}) = \text{Ph}_{11} \text{Ph}_{11} \text{Ph}_{411} \text{Ph}_{31}$
   $= (\pm\text{adv} \pm\text{Aux} +\text{Mn} \pm\text{Md} \pm\text{r})$
   $(\pm\text{i} \pm\text{q} +\text{H} \pm\text{A} \pm\text{d}) (+\text{R} +\text{Ax}) (+\text{U} +\text{Or})$.

[28] See also Zvelebil. "How to Handle the Structure of Tamil", *Archiv Orientálni*, 30,116-42.

5. $\mathscr{R}$ ($\pm$adv $\pm$Aux $+$Mn $\pm$Md $\pm$r) = adv Aux Mn.

6. $\mathscr{R}$ ($\pm$i $\pm$q $+$H $\pm$A $\pm$d) = HAd.

7. $\mathscr{R}$ ($+$R $+$ Ax) = R Ax.

8. $\mathscr{R}$ ($+$U $+$Or) = U Or.

9. $\mathscr{E}$ (adv Aux Mn) = $a^5\textit{P}$ ('already') W_{5aux} W_5.

10. $\mathscr{E}$ (HAd) = Noun Adjective dq^3h ('a certain').

11. $\mathscr{E}$ (R Ax) = ri^3ki^3 ('under') Ph_{11}.

12. $\mathscr{E}$ (U Or) = gwi^3 ('day') Ph_{61}.

13. Substitution of 9-12 in the string obtained by 4. with removal of parentheses:

    $a^5\textit{P}\,W_{5aux}\,W_5$ Noun Adjective dq^3h
    ri^3ki^3 Ph_{11} gwi^3 Ph_{61}.

14. $\mathscr{R}$ (W_{5aux}) = $\mathscr{R}$ ($+$asp $+$mood $+$vs$'_{aux}$) = (asp mood vs$'_{aux}$).

15. $\mathscr{R}$ (W_5) = $\mathscr{R}$ ($+$asp $+$mood $+$vs$'$) = (asp mood vs$'$).

16. $\mathscr{R}$ (Ph_{11}) = $\mathscr{R}$ ($\pm$i $\pm$q $+$H $\pm$A $\pm$d) = (H d).

17. $\mathscr{E}$ (H d) = (Noun dq^3h).

18. $\mathscr{R}$ (Ph_{61}) = $\mathscr{R}$ ($\pm$m $+$sc $\pm$int) = sc int.

19. Substituting 14-18 in the string obtained in 13.; removal of parentheses:

    $a^5\textit{P}$ asp-mood-vs$'_{aux}$ asp-mood-vs$'$
    Noun Adjective dq^3h ri^3ki^3 Noun
    dq^3h gwi^3 sc int.

20. Lexical substitution by resort to a cross reference dictionary:

    $a^5\textit{P}$ $gq^3\textit{P}q^{34}h$ $ga^5wi^5\textit{P}$ $\check{z}u^3we^3$ ga^5ci^5 dq^3h
    ri^3ki^3 $\check{c}\mu^3$ dq^3h gwi^3 go^4 $gq^5\textit{P}q^3h$.

'Already went to die that white dog under that box the twenty-fourth day.'

I

CLAUSE LEVEL PROCEDURES

1. PRELIMINARY PROCEDURES FOR CLAUSE LEVEL ANALYSIS

1.0. Definition of clause: a class of syntagmemes of a median hierarchical order ranking above such syntagmemes as the phrase and word and below such syntagmemes as the sentence and discourse. It may be non-centered, centered, or relator-axis. Non-centered clauses express some such meaning as predication or equation. Centered clauses expand a predication given in a predicate phrase or word. Relator-axis clauses are imbedded in another clause or in a phrase by means of an overt relator.

In essence, the clause posits a situation in miniature (whether asserting, questioning, commanding, or equating). Predication clauses, in particular, have a tagmeme expressing the PLOT (normally manifested by some verb-like structure), one or more tagmemes expressing DRAMATIS PERSONAE (e.g. actor, goal, indirect object), and other tagmemes contributing PROPS, SCENERY, and LOCAL COLOR (e.g. instrument, location, manner, and time). Equation clauses equate some entity with another entity either by means of an overt copula (English: *God is judge*) or without a copula (Hebrew: *dɔn ʔlohim* 'God [is] judge').

In non-centered clauses predication is not expressed within the predicate tagmeme itself which has no bound subject. Rather the predicate, unmarked for subject, is juxtaposed to a subject expressed by another clause level tagmeme. This is true of English and of Trique.

In some language, however, clauses are centered constructions. Such languages contain bound subjects within their predicates and such subjects must occur whether or not a substantive phrase also expresses subject elsewhere in the clause. The predicate tagmeme in such a language may, in fact, mark not only the subject, but further categories such as object, indirect object, and instruments. Such a predicate tagmeme functions as a center expanded by epexegetical elements elsewhere in the clause; it is a text upon which the sermon, the whole clause, is built. Consider the following Zoque (transitive) clause *nakšah ʔʌ yʌʔki te tuhkuhiʔŋ* 'they-me-hit me here a gun-with', i.e. 'they hit me here with a gun'. In this clause *nakšah* is a Zoque transitive verb manifesting predicate tagmeme. In that it is unmarked by a prefix it indicates third person acting on first person. The clause-in-miniature is further amplified by *ʔʌ* 'me' which manifests object tagmeme, *yʌʔki* 'here' which manifests locative tagmeme and *te tuhkuhiʔŋ* 'with a gun' which manifests instrumental-accompaniment.

Quiché affords an even more striking example of centered clauses. In the following clause the predicate tagmeme *k-eb-u-lu-kʔam lok* 'present-them-he-for-bring this-way', i.e. 'he brings them this way for (somebody)' is the center of a clause whose other tagmemes amplify its predicate:

manuel	kebulukʔam	lok	ri	šila	čke	pa	ri
'Manuel	brings		hither	the	chairs	for-them	into the
ha	čanim						
house	immediately'						

Fox diagrams the relationships as follows:

Subject Predicate Object Indirect Referent Location Time

Clause: *manuel kebulukʔam lok ri šila čke pa ri ha čanim*

Predicate Tagmeme: *k-eb-u-lu-kʔam lok*

Aspect/Time	Object	Subject	Benefactive	Stem	Directional
(present)	(them)	(he)	(for)	(bring)	(this way)

The fact that the word may constitute a minimal clause in some languages in no way invalidates the distinction between clause and word. While similar tagmemes may occur in both the verb-like word and the predication clause, other word types (e.g., noun, adjective, numeral) and other clause types (non-verbal) usually exist as well. Furthermore, a comparison of even elaborate verb structures (e.g., Candoshi, Quechua, Eskimo) with clauses reveals that the two levels of organization differ in relative regidity and expandibility as well as in the amount of information conveyed by their constituent tagmemes (cf. 9.0.).

Relator-axis clauses have a bipartite structure which consists of a subordinating conjunction, particle, or phrase (the relator) followed by a sequence (the axis) which is structurally identical with (or a recognizable variant of) one or more clause types posited elsewhere. The relator may be a functional specialization of some clause level tagmeme. Thus, *when I first came here*, *where you went*, *on which I stand*, and *which I purchased yesterday* are all relator-axis clauses in English; their relator tagmemes are manifested by specialized functions of temporal, locational, and object tagmemes respectively. As specialized functors, *when*, *where*, *on which*, and *which* serve to relate their clauses within the framework of an imbedding clause or phrase. Thus, *when I first came here he was gone* has an overall structure temporal-subject-predicate; the imbedded clause *when I first came here* manifests the first tagmeme (temporal) of the imbedding clause. Likewise, *I will never forget that evil hour when I first came here* is a clause of actor-predicate-object structure. The last clause level tagmeme is manifested by a noun phrase (*that evil hour when I first came here*) which contains an imbedded clause (*when I first came here*).

Relator-axis clauses are structurally similar to relator-axis (prepositional) phrases. Typically, a prepositional phrase consists of a preposition plus a noun phrase. In spite of structural distinctions among noun phrase types, it is commonly found that any one of a variety of noun phrases may fill the axis slot in a relator-axis phrase, while the presence of the relator sets up a pronounced immediate constituent layering which brackets off the relator (preposition) from everything that follows. Thus, the following three sequences presumably manifest structurally distinct noun phrase types in

English: *the Puritan's Boston, historical old Boston,* and *Boston, one of our oldest cities.* Nevertheless, any of these sequences may manifest axis tagmeme in a relator-axis phrase such as *in historical old Boston.* Furthermore, whatever the sequence manifesting axis tagmeme, the immediate constituent layering is such that such prepositions as *in* are bracketed off from all that follows.

Similarly, in spite of structural differences among clause types they indifferently fill the axis slot in relator-axis clauses, while the presence of a (often preposed) subordinator sets up an immediate constitutent layering in which the subordinator is bracketed off from all that follows it. Thus, in comparing axis-related phrases and axis-related clauses the following parallelism is seen:

$$\frac{\text{preposition}}{\text{following noun phrase}} = \frac{\text{subordinator}}{\text{following clause}}$$

In some languages relator-axis clauses are formally marked in other ways besides the addition of a subordinator. Thus, the predicate of a relator-axis clause may be formally distinct from that of an independent clause (see Zoque subordinate clauses 2.3. and 2.4.). In some languages subordinate clauses are formally less extensive and less elaborate than independent clauses.

Thus, in searching for clauses we begin by looking for strings containing a subject and predicate whether both are expressed by free forms or whether the former is bound to the latter. Our search will not, however, necessarily stop here. Within a given language we may find sequences which lack a subject, but which are otherwise distributionally parallel to sequences recognized as clauses. English has an imperative clause in which no subject occurs. Trique has a meteorological clause likewise without a subject: *ga³mą³⁵ʔ* 'rained', *ži³gį³⁵* 'dawned' (rather than the illogical English idiom *it rained* and *it dawned*). Nevertheless, these sequences in both languages, in spite of the omission of a subject, pattern like clauses in respect to occurrence with them of other clause level tagmemes. Thus, the English *Fire!* may be expanded to *Fire this gun at once towards the stated objective,* while the Trique *ga³mą³⁵ʔ* 'rained' may be expanded to *ga³mą³⁵ʔ ma³ka²¹ gu³kï³* 'rained in Mexico City yesterday'.

Apart from omission of subject in such clauses as those just described there may be omission of subject in sufficient linguistic or situational context. Compare the English: *Went down to the lake front yesterday. Caught a fine mess of bass. Wish you were here too.* In this particular context – scenic postcard with short message and signature *Harry* – the subject may be omitted.

Many languages contain certain clause-like structures containing as center some verb derived form similar to what is called infinitive, gerund, or participle in European languages. Not only do these clause-like structures differ from clauses in respect to external distribution and function (as adjectives and substantive) but often they also omit a subject as well. In that their internal structure is on the whole similar to that of the clause in such languages it may prove convenient to analyze them as further type(s) of clause structure stateable usually in terms of transform rule(s).

1.1. Isolate clause units in text by drawing bars at clause boundaries. Bracket clause fragments that do not seem to constitute clauses and/or which involve sequences in which it seems difficult to demarcate one clause from another. Avoid extremes of (a) bracketing too many data and (b) failing to bracket data which present genuine difficulties. The first extreme may reduce one's corpus to a size smaller than is adequate, while the second extreme may introduce data too complex for initial analysis. Bracketed data will be reckoned with later under procedure 4.1.

Encircle any clause that nests within another clause: /*The boy who came yesterday* didn't stay long/. This whole unit (including the encircled clause) is isolable as a clause. Similarly the encircled clause itself is isolable.

1.2. Copy each clause on a 3 × 5 or 4 × 6 filing slip with translation (if the latter is necessary for your handling of the data) and accurate reference to the location in your corpus.

Make a rough, etic analysis of the clause on each file slip by jotting over or under the line such symbols as A (for actor), P (for predicate), G (for goal), S (for subject), I (for indirect object), In (for instrument), L (for location), D (for direction), T (for time), M (for manner), C (for cause), and the like. Or it may be more advantageous to use a non-committal type of notation that partially summarizes the formal features of a recognizable slot. For example, in my pilot study of Hebrew, certain tagmas were roughly labeled as follows: 1- + per. n (personal noun), b- + temp. n (temporal noun), N + loc. s (noun + locative suffix).

At least 200 slips should be accumulated as the corpus for even a modest pilot study. For serious study of the clause structure of a language a corpus of at least 1000 slips is recommended.

The purpose of this preliminary procedure and the three following procedures is to isolate clause level tagmas – clause segments which consist of function-set correlations tentatively identified by the analyst and labeled for future analysis. Some tagmas identified here and in the following preliminary procedures will prove on analysis to be tagmemes as well (see 3.1.) but other tagmas will need to be grouped, on the basis of non-contrastive distribution, into tagmemes according to the procedures of section 3.

This procedure requires that one recognize sequences of words (or morphemes) that together fill one clause level function slot (e.g., *the big brown bear* in *I saw the big brown bear yesterday*). In that the internal analysis of such sequences belongs to word and/or phrase structure no analysis of them as such need be made under clause structure. A knowledge of word and/or phrase structure is, of course, of considerable advantage when available. Nevertheless, practical considerations of work programming often may make it desirable to postpone detailed analysis of phrase structure until later. It is usually necessary, however, at one or more points in clause analysis to anticipate certain matters of word and/or phrase structure that are relevant to the manifestation of clause level tagmemes. This is true whenever an identifying-contrastive feature of one or more clause level tagmemes is (a) a given morpheme or (b) a characteristic word or phrase type, or (c) a bound form which occurs in an either-or relationship with a free form as manifestation of a clause level tagmeme.

The case endings of Latin or Greek illustrate well situation (a) above. It is of course the rule that a given case ending has a variety of functions (e.g. Latin, where the accusative case ending marks direct object, predicate accusative, extent, and duration – to mention four clause level functions). Somewhat similar is the function of Hebrew *l-* and *b-* in distinguishing clause level tagmemes in Hebrew (with *l-* marking indirect object, role, temporal, and purpose; and with *b-* marking instrumental, locational, and temporal). Malayo-Polynesian languages typically use an ensemble of phrase-initial particles which serve partially to distinguish from each other certain clause level tagmemes. Markers of the sort illustrated here for Indo-European, Semitic, and Malayo-Polynesian only rarely constitute unambiguous markers of clause level tagmemes. Nevertheless these, together with other considerations (word order, manifesting set, cross reference and lexical probability) comprise identifying contrastive features of such tagmemes. Our analysis must therefore take account of such word level and phrase level features even when we are focusing specifically on the clause level.

Similarly, (b) a characteristic phrase formation may be an identifying-contrastive feature of a tagmeme in a given language. Thus, in Trique, the relator-axis phrase is a special phrase type (with relator tagmeme manifested by eleven words most of which are nouns that refer to body parts but are used here in a prepositional-like function) that in the predication clause occurs as manifestation of location, temporal, and instrumental tagmemes. Without recognition of this special diagnostic phrase type the description of Trique clause level tagmemes would be difficult in that object tagmeme and location tagmeme could not so readily be shown to be different.

Situation (c) above is well illustrated in Ixil where there are bound forms (termed by Elliott post-clitics) that occur either as subject of intransitive verb or object of transitive verb. In either situation, however, the post-clitic subject or object does not occur if a free noun expression manifests either tagmeme: *kat-ul-i stoh* 'past-came-he afoot", i.e. 'he came afoot' and *kat-ul u nah stoh* 'the man came afoot' – in which the post-clitic -*i* 'he' and *u nah* 'the man' are mutually exclusive. Consequently, the post-clitics belong to a class of substantive expressions manifesting clause level subject in one clause type and clause level object in the other. The fact that these post-clitics are phonologically bound should not be permitted to obscure the fact that they manifest clause level tagmemes. Furthermore, in that these post-clitics are the outermost layer of suffixal-like elements in the phonological complex centering around the verb, they may easily be peeled off grammatically without disturbing the internal grammatical relationships of the word-phrase level elements in the verb itself.

In another Mayan language of Guatemala, K'ekchi', we must, however, proceed more cautiously in this respect. K'ekchi' has a series of pronominal prefixes (Series A) which manifests subject of semi-transitive verb (corresponding roughly to the intransitive verb of Ixil) and goal of transitive verb. In the K'ekchi' semi-transitive verb – unlike Ixil – this pronominal element is an obligatory word-phrase level tagmeme that must occur whether or not a substantive expression manifesting clause level subject tagmeme also occurs in the same clause. In this situation we set up a word-phrase level subject tagmeme and a clause level subject tagmeme as well (with the latter epexegetical of the former). But in the transitive verb where this same pronoun series manifests goal, the situation is more complex. While a goal tagma of some sort must occur in a K'ekchi' transitive clause it may be either a word-phrase level element, i.e., a pronominal prefix of Series A, or a clause level element, i.e., a substantive expression.

K'ekchi' Semi-transitive Clause:
(+ pronoun A   + verb stem) ±substantive expression
manifesting subject   manifesting subject

K'ekchi' Transitive clause:

$$\overline{\hspace{2.5cm}/\hspace{3cm}}$$

(± pronoun A + pronoun B + verb stem) ± substantive expression
manifesting   manifesting   manifesting goal
goal   subject

Here we have a situation of mutual exclusion that is reminiscent of the Ixil data described above. Nevertheless, in K'ekchi' we have set up goal manifested by prefix as a word-phrase level tagmeme and goal manifested by substantive expression as a clause level tagmeme – with mention that the two tagmemes are mutually exclusive as to manifestation. This decision is based on two considerations: (1) It seems like reckless surgery to cut out and assign to clause structure such a morpheme as *at-* 'you' (pronominal series A) from a form such as *t-at-š-toh* 'he will pay you' (*toh* verb stem, 'to pay') when it is bracketed by elements (*t-* 'future tense indicator' and *š-* 'he' pronoun series B) that seem unequivocally to manifest word level tagmemes. (2) In that pronoun series A seems clearly to manifest a word-phrase level subject tagmeme in semi-transitive verbs it seems reasonable to believe that it also manifests a word-phrase level goal tagmeme in transitive.

1.3. File the slips in some fashion so as to bring together at one spot in the file all examples of clauses having the same filler of predicate slot (by this is meant same verb stem or noun stem in predicate slot plus or minus different accompanying affixes, particles, or auxiliary verbs). In languages where stems are relatively unchanging the filing may be carried out by simply alphabetizing according to filler of the predicate. In languages where stems have several forms filing may be carried out according to (a) a hypothetical basic form, (b) an actually occurring stem-variant consistently chosen as basic – even if only for filing purposes, or (c) according to translation gloss (with a certain inevitable inconsistency in filing in the latter case).

While this step may not be too profitable if the corpus is small, it is of considerable usefulness in handling a corpus approximating the size here recommended. This procedure provides, in effect, a case study of each lexical item manifesting a predicate tagma in respect to what tagmas may occur with it. It is from these individual painstaking case studies of particular lexical selections in tentatively identified slots that grammatical statements are to be deduced. Furthermore, in that the selection of items manifesting one tagma versus another tagma is based on principles as yet unknown to the investigator, a study of the particular selections of a given verb with given lexical items manifesting subject, object, instrumental, temporal, locational, and the like, leads to greater accuracy in listing items manifesting each. In that this last statement may appear enigmatic, a detailed illustration follows.

It soon becomes evident in filing Trique clauses that there is some sort of object tagma (which occurs with great statistical frequency following the actor and the initial predicate) as well as a locational tagma (which occurs with great statistical frequency out beyond the object). In such a clause as $a^3\check{c}a^{21}$ zi^3 $\text{?}ngo^4$ $\check{c}a\text{?}a^3$ ri^3q^{34} ne^3h gwi^{354} 'sings he a song before the people' ($a^3\check{c}a^{21}$ 'sings', zi^3 'he', $\text{?}ngo^4$ $\check{c}a\text{?}a^3$ 'a song', ri^3q^{34} ne^3h gwi^{354} 'before the people') it is easy to identify $\text{?}ngo^4$ $\check{c}a\text{?}a^3$ 'a song' as manifesting object tagma and ri^3q^{34} ne^3h gwi^{354} 'before the people' as locational. But in such a clause as $gq^3\text{?}q^{34}h$ dre^{23} $k\ddot{\imath}h\ddot{\imath}^3$ 'went father-my mountain', i.e. 'my father went to the mountain', it is difficult to know whether from the standpoint of the tagmemic structure of Trique $k\ddot{\imath}h\ddot{\imath}^3$ 'mountain' should be considered to be an object or a locational. The mere fact that the verb go does not take an object in English must not be allowed to determine our decision. Furthermore, a single noun may occur not only in object but in locational as well, as in the following clause: gi^3ri^{34} zi^3 $da^3\text{?}ni^{21}$ ma^3ystru^{23} $du^3gwa^3ga\text{?}a^{43}$ 'withdrew he son-of schoolteacher (from) jail', i.e. 'he drew the son of the schoolteacher out of jail', where $du^3gwa^3ga\text{?}a^{43}$ 'jail' which occurs after the object seems clearly to manifest locational tagma. The question therefore remains: Granted that object and locational are distinguishable tagmas both of which will probably prove to be tagmemes, nevertheless, when but one noun expression occurs out beyond the predicate and actor tagmas in a clause involving a verb such as $gq^3\text{?}q^{34}h$ 'went', then is this further tagma to be identified as object or as locational?

Precisely in quandaries of this sort information deduced from a corpus filed as here suggested proves helpful. Specifically, it is found that $gq^3\text{?}q^{34}h$ 'went' (or its other aspect $wq^3\text{?}q^{34}h$ 'going') plus a noun manifesting actor occurs with items such as the following: (a) relator-axis phrases: $ne^{34}\text{?}$ $da^3\text{-}zdu^3ne^3$ 'towards Yosonduchi', ri^3q^{34} do^3kto^2r 'before the doctor', nda^{43} do^3yo^3h 'as far as Juxtlahuaca', $zi^3\text{-}ga^3n\ddot{\imath}^2h$ $koho^3$ 'among the bushes', and ri^3ki^3 $koho^3$ 'under the bushes'; (b) place names: nga^3h 'Putla', ni^3gq^2 'Tlaxiaco', $go^3ba^3la^{23}$ 'Copala', $zq^3mi^3ge^2$ 'San Miguel'; and (c) items of the sort which have caused us classificatory difficulty, viz: $kihi^3$ 'mountains', $du^3gwa^3zo^{43}$ 'the town hall', nu^2wi^3 'the church', ze^2nda^3 'the hacienda'. Once itemized in this fashion it is not difficult to see that these various items and constructions manifest locational tagma. Relator-axis phrases of the sort listed under (a) manifest only locational tagma, never actor or object, while place names of the sort listed under (b) only with great rarity manifest actor or object tagmas but frequently manifest locational. Group (c) in which $kihi^3$ 'mountain' occurs is found to act much like (b). The above summary statements are based on data in which object and locational occur in sequence and are unambiguously identified by word order. The list of items occurring with $wq^3\text{?}q^{34}h/gq^3\text{?}q^{34}h$ 'go' contains then a group of items (a), which never manifests object when object is unambiguously identifiable, and further groups of items, (b) and (c), that only with great statistical rarity manifest object in such an unambiguous situation but with considerable frequency are found manifesting locational. If we assume, then, that the verb $wq^3\text{?}q^{34}h/gq^3\text{?}q^{34}h$ 'go' displays any consistency as to selection of tagmas that occur with it in the same clause, it seems clear that $kihi^3$ 'mountain' in the clause above must be considered to manifest locational. Notice, however, that aside from some such a technique as that here suggested, it would be all too easy to confuse the items manifesting object and locational so that the structural difference between the two tagmas (and between, eventually, two tagmemes) would be obscured.

Relator-axis clauses may be filed according to the lexical items manifesting the relator tagma. Thus, English relator-axis clauses may be filed alphabetically under such relators as: *that, when, where, which, who, whom.*

1.4. **Make a guess as to the number of separate charts that will handle the data well.** Considerable confusion may be avoided if one does not attempt to chart all clause types on the same chart. Such distinctions as the following often prove relevant: Predication versus equation, transitive versus intransitive versus ditransitive (with two objects), active versus passive, nominal clause versus verbal clause, indicative versus imperative versus interrogative. Certain of these distinctions may determine sub-types rather than main types; other distinctions (e.g., indicative versus interrogative versus imperative) sometimes prove relevant on the sentence level rather than on the clause level. Relator-axis (subordinate) clauses should be charted separately. An unnecessary subdivision of a chart into two charts does no harm here in that all suspect types are scrutinized in the procedures of section 2. Likewise, an inadvertent charting together of two distinct types should also be detectable by later procedures. In fact, the very process of charting often uncovers such errors.

1.5. Copy the data from the filing slips onto charts: (a) There should be a column for each tagma, i.e. for each tentatively identified function-set correlation (there will need to be a residue column for items not classifiable as yet). (b) Columns should be arranged in the statistically most common ordering of the tagmas – if such an ordering can be posited. Where the order of the columns indicates a statistically common ordering of tagmas, departures from this order may be indicated by drawing arrows. (c) Columns can be arranged in an arbitrary order if no particular order seems to be statistically prominent. In this event subscript numbers can be used to record the linear order. (d) Needless to say, a chart may need to include a succession of pages to accomodate all the data.

Thus, the Trique clause $a^3\check{c}a^{21}$ zi^3 ngo^4 $\check{c}a\mathit{P}a^3$ ri^3q^{34} ne^3h gwi^{354} 'sings he a song before the people' would be transferred to a chart as follows:

P	S	O	L	T	Residue
$a^3\check{c}a^{21}$	zi^3	ngo^4 $\check{c}a\mathit{P}a^3$	ri^3q^{34} ne^3h gwi^{354}		
'sings'	'he'	'a song'	'before the people'		

In some languages characterized by comparatively free word order it may still be possible to obtain clues to tagmemic structure by observing relative sequence in accordance with the following: (a) Analyze at first only clauses with the statistically most prominent word order, e.g. verb clauses with initial verb in Hebrew. (b) Further narrow the corpus to clauses maintaining a few pivotal tagmas in the same order, e.g., to clauses with the order predicate-actor-object in Hebrew. (c) Analyze relative order of other tagmas in the narrowed corpus. (d) After applying the procedures of sections 2 and 3 to the narrower corpus, check results against an unrestricted corpus. You should be able to recognize the same tagmas already identified in that while the order of elements will be freer in the larger corpus nevertheless other criteria will remain (e.g. criteria of cross reference, manifesting set, and manifesting constructions, as given below).

2. ANALYTICAL PROCEDURES FOR CLAUSE LEVEL SYNTAGMEMES, I.E. FOR CLAUSE TYPES

It is assumed that an analysis of clause level tagmemes is in process but not necessarily complete. We search, therefore, for structural differences among the tagmas of one sort of clause that is suspect of being emically distinct from another sort of clause.

Two clause types are syntagmemically distinct if (a) there be at least two structural differences between them, and (b) at least one of these differences involve the nuclear and/or obligatory tagmas. The distinction nucleus versus periphery is of relevance to clause types in most languages. When relevant the nucleus may be distinguished from the periphery in accordance with the criteria set forth in 2.1. When not relevant to the description of a given language, the distinction nucleus versus periphery should be replaced with that of obligatory versus optional.

Structural differences distinguishing clause types are as follows: (a) an obligatory difference in the ordering of similar elements, or a marked statistical preference for different ordering of such elements; (b) a different internal structuring of sequences manifesting clause level tagmas, i.e. differences in the structure of words, phrases, and subordinate clauses; (c) a difference in emic classes manifesting two tagmas (by definition an emic class is not set up here *ad hoc* but reflects a distinction useful at some other point in the grammar); (d) a difference in the number of tagmas in one type versus the other; presence of a given tagma in one type versus its absence in the other;

(e) a regularly stateable grammatical transform. (a) above is illustrated by the Ixil example described under 2.4. where two clause types each with two obligatory clause level tagmas have a different mutual ordering of the predicate tagmas in reference to the other obligatory tagma in each clause: $+P_1 +S$ versus $+Ag +P_3$. In Trique one clause type (the transitive predication clause) has a marked statistical preference for the order predicate, actor, object, while another clause type (which is eventually termed the equation clause) has a marked statistical preference for the order subject, equative, complement. (b) above is also illustrated by the Trique clause types just cited. While in the predication clause actor and object are restricted in that they are not manifested by relator-axis or temporal phrases, subject and complement tagmemes are not so restricted but may be manifested both by noun phrases and also by phrases of the other two types. (c) above is illustrated by transitive versus intransitive verbs in a number of languages (e.g., K'ekchi', Zoque, and Cashibo). (d) above is illustrated by possible presence of object in one clause type versus absence of object in another in both English and Trique. (e) above is illustrated by the fact that while the English transitive clauses (e.g., *I drove the car*) may be transformed to passive, other clauses which contain intransitive verbs may not be so transformed.

The following procedures are stated in terms of tagmemes rather than tagmas in that it is the solid and enduring contrasts that ultimately are significant in distinguishing clause types.

2.1. Identify the nuclear (versus peripheral) tagmemes for each variety of clause charted. In identifying nuclear tagmas the following criteria are useful, but all are not necessarily relevant to clause structure in a given language:

(1) All obligatory tagmemes are nuclear (although not all nuclear tagmemes are obligatory). Thus, in all English clause types except the imperative, both subject and predicate (defining predicate as the verb and its immediate modifiers – excluding objects and complements) are obligatory. In the English copulative clause, subject, predicate, and complement are all obligatory and hence nuclear. By this criterion or by (4), relator tagmemes (subordinating

conjunctions, particles, or phrases) are nuclear to relator-axis clauses. Peripheral tagmemes are optional.

(2) Tagmemes in agreement with the predicate (which is typically the CORE tagmeme) or in explicit cross reference to it, are nuclear. Thus, the English subject tagmeme is seen to be nuclear by virtue of the fact that third person subjects agree with a present tense verb in respect to number. This agreement is much more explicit in classical languages where person and number of verb agree throughout with the person and number of the subject. In Hebrew, verbs are inflected to indicate person, number, and gender of subject. In all these instances this feature of agreement marks subject tagmemes as nuclear. Similarly, in some languages person and number of object or of indirect object are indicated in the verb – thus formally marking the nuclear status of clause level object tagmeme.

In Mikasuki (Seminole) action clauses (of which there are four types), not only are subject, object, and indirect object nuclear, but also instrumental and space. Subject is indicated by -ot on the end of the subject nominal which agrees with the subject suffix in the verb manifesting predicate. Nominals manifesting other non-subject functions are marked with -on. Direct object and indirect object agree with prefixes in the verb manifesting predicate. Presence of a clause level instrumental tagmeme is signalled by a cross reference feature, prefix s-/is-, in the verb while presence of clause level space tagmeme is signalled by one of six prefixes in the verb. *ahon s-im-bakahlom i:fon* 'stick (he)-instrument-indirect object-threw dog', i.e., 'he threw a stick at the dog'. Clause level instrumental tagmeme is manifested by *ahon*; clause level predicate, by *simbakahlom*; and clause level indirect object by *i:fon*. Within the predicate itself, *s-* cross references to the instrumental; and *im-* indicates third person singular indirect object (third person singular subject is unmarked).

> *bakson   ahon   a-yofihlom*
> 'rope   tree   (he)-ties-to'

i.e., 'He ties the rope to a tree'. *bakson* and *ahon* manifest clause level direct object and space tagmemes respectively and are cross referenced to in the verb by unmarked third person object and *a*-space prefix.

(3) Nuclear tagmemes tend to occur contiguously to each other in some languages. Thus, in the Trique transitive predication clause, predicate, subject, and object are nuclear. Predicate and subject are invariably contiguous to each other. Object occurs separated from predicate and subject only with great rarity.

(4) Some nuclear tagmemes are limited to particular clause types; peripheral tagmemes tend to occur indifferently in various clause types.

(5) Nuclear tagmemes may be affected by transformations between clause types or between a clause type and some other construction; peripheral tagmemes are not. Thus, in English active and passive clauses, subject, predicate, direct object, indirect object, and agent are all seen to be nuclear. (a) *The teacher gave John a book.* (b) *John was given a book by the teacher.* (c) *A book was given John by the teacher.* In (a) subject is manifested by *teacher*; predicate by *gave*; indirect object by *John*; and direct object by *a book*. But the subject of (a) is transformed to agent in (b) and (c). The active predicate of (a) is transformed to a passive predicate in (b) and (c). *John*, indirect object in (a) and (c) becomes subject in (b); while *book*, direct object in (a) and (b) becomes subject in (c). All these tagmemes are affected by the transforms and hence are nuclear. But clause (a) could be expanded by adding words like *yesterday*, and *right in the schoolroom* – manifesting temporal and locational respectively. These words, without shift of function can also occur in (b) and (c). Locational and temporal are therefore peripheral and not nuclear in these English clause types.

(6) Nuclear tagmemes may be marked by special case endings or particles in some languages. This criterion usually is ancillary to the preceding. Thus, in Maranao, predicate tagmemes (marked for one of four voices) enter into a well-elaborated system of cross reference with clause level subject, object, referent, and instrumental tagmemes. When a predicate tagmeme is manifested by a verb in subjective voice then the subject nominal manifests subject-as-topic and is introduced by the particle *so*. When a predicate tagmeme is

manifested by a verb in one of the other three voices then subject nominals manifest subject tagmeme and are introduced by the particle *o*. When a predicate tagmeme is manifested by a verb in objective voice, then the object nominal manifests object-as-topic and is likewise introduced by the particle *so*; otherwise object nominals manifest object tagmeme and are introduced by the particle *sa* (or by *ko* in the instrumental voice.) Likewise, a verb in referential voice takes referent-as-topic tagmeme introduced by *so* while verbs in other voices take a referent tagmeme introduced by *ko* (or by *sa* in the instrumental voice). Finally, verbs in instrumental voice take instrument-as-topic tagmeme introduced by *so*; otherwise instrument tagmeme introduced by *ko* occurs. These relations are summarized in the following diagram of McKaughan's:

VOICE	SUBJECT	OBJECT	REFERENT	INSTRUMENT
1. Subjective	*so*- phrase	*sa*- phrase	*ko*- phrase	
2. Objective	*o*- phrase	*so*- phrase	*ko*- phrase	*ko*- phrase
3. Referential	*o*- phrase	*sa*- phrase	*so*- phrase	*ko*- phrase
4. Instrumental	*o*- phrase	*sa*- or *ko*- phrase	*sa*- or *ko*- phrase	*so*- phrase

Subject, object, referent, instrument as well as the four corresponding topic tagmemes – occurring in a diagonal down the chart – are overtly marked as nuclear in highly systematic fashion. They are also seen to be nuclear by virtue of cross reference to the predicate tagmemes (choice of voice), and by their involvement in transforms between the four clause types.

(7) In that nucleus versus periphery is emic to clauses in a given language, judgments made on the basis of such criteria as (1)-(6) just given, must be subject to subsequent review in the light of overall relevance. Specifically, tagmemes are labelled as nuclear if they in general conform to criteria of the sort here suggested and if such a labelling proves useful in distinguishing clause types.[1]

2.2 Separate as different clause types any two varieties which have at least a difference of two in the number of nuclear tagmemes.

[1] Languages are recursive systems and analysis of the sort here suggested is not to be brushed aside as circular reasoning simply because it reflects the recursiveness of language itself.

By this procedure the Zoque intransitive clause is readily seen to be syntagmemically distinct from the Zoque ditransitive clause, as seen in the following nuclear formulae:

$$\text{Intr. Cl: } (+Pi \pm S)$$
$$\text{Ditr. Cl: } (+Pt_2 \pm A \pm O_1 \pm O_2)$$

In the above formulae, S (subject), A (actor), O_1 (first object), and O_2 (second object) are all nuclear to their clause types as seen in the fact that (a) the verb person-number prefixes cross-reference to these tagmemes, (b) they tend to remain closer to the predicate tagmeme than do the others and occur more frequently. The occurrence of two nuclear tagmemes in the intransitive clause versus four nuclear tagmemes in the ditransitive easily distinguishes them as separate clause types.

2.3. Separate as different clause types any two varieties which have a difference of one in the number of nuclear tagmemes provided that a further structural difference is present.

Zoque intransitive clauses and transitive clauses have the following nuclear formulae:

$$\text{Intr. Cl.: } (+P_1 \pm S)$$
$$\text{Tr. Cl.: } (+P_t \pm A \pm O)$$

The count of the nuclear tagmemes in these two varieties of clause establishes one difference: two nuclear tagmemes versus three. A second structural difference is easily found: Actor (A) of the transitive clause is distinct from subject (S) of the intransitive in that the former has a case-marking suffix $-Ps \sim -Pis$ which the latter does not have. Further differences could also be found, viz. special patterns of derivation for verbs manifesting transitive predicate; and occurrence of accompaniment tagmeme in intransitive clauses versus instrumental-accompaniment in transitive clauses.

Zoque transitive clause may be separated from the ditransitive clause by this same procedure:

$$\text{Tr. Cl.: } (+P_t \pm A \pm O)$$
$$\text{Ditr. Cl.: } (+P_{t_2} \pm A \pm O_1 \pm O_2)$$

Not only is there a different number of nuclear tagmemes in these two clause types, but further differences may be cited as well: (1) ditransitive verbs may be derived from transitive verbs; (2) the function of the person-number prefix is different (as seen by cross reference to A and O in transitive but to A, O_1 and O_2 in ditransitive).

Zoque subordinate clauses contrast with indicative clauses (crisscrossing matrix-wise the contrast of intransitive, transitive, and ditransitive). Specifically, an intransitive indicative clause contrasts with an intransitive subordinate clause as seen in the following nuclear formulae:

$$\text{Intr. Ind.: } (+P_1 \pm S)$$
$$\text{Intr. Sub.: } (\pm sb +P_{1s} \pm S)$$

The subordinate clause may be optionally introduced by subordinator such as *komo* or *huc* 'as', *kwando* or *deke* 'when', or *hut* 'where'. Although optional, subordinator tagmeme is nuclear in that it is diagnostic of its clause type. Thus, the two clause types. are separated by one difference. A second difference is seen in the fact that a subordinate predicate is optionally marked by one of a class of subordinating suffixes, e.g. *-se* 'manner subordinative', *-mʌ* 'locative subordinative', and *-ʔk* 'temporal subordinative'.

English active transitive and active intransitive clauses differ in respect to the presence of three nuclear tagmemes in the first type versus two in the second:

$$\text{Act. Tr. Cl.: } (+S +P_a \pm O)$$
$$\text{Act. Intr. Cl.: } (+S +P_a)$$

On inspection it appears that the only overt difference between the two clause types is the occurrence of a third nuclear tagmeme (object) in the active transitive. A second difference, however, is seen in the fact that the active transitive clause may be transformed to passive while the active intransitive has no such transform.

2.4. Separate as different clause types any two varieties which have the same number of nuclear tagmemes, provided that at least two nuclear tagmemes in one type contrast with two nuclear tagmemes in the other type.

Nuclear formulae for the Trique transitive predicative clause and the equative clause follow:

$$\text{Tr. Cl.: } (+P_t +A \pm O)$$
$$\text{Eq. Cl.: } (+S +P_e +C)$$

Both clause types contain a predicate, (labelled transitive predicate in one and equative predicate in the other); both also contain some sort of subject (labelled actor in one and subject in the other); and finally both contain a further element (labelled object in one and complement in the other). Yet it can be shown that each of these pairs of tagmemes contrast. The contrast of transitive versus equative predicators is part of a broader pattern of contrast among transitive, intransitive, and equative (copulative) verbs – a contrast relevant to the structure of both clauses and phrases (hence not *ad hoc* and hence countable here as a structural contrast). Actor contrasts with subject in that the latter may be manifested by relator-axis (prepositional phrases) and subordinate clauses of a type never found to manifest actor. In similar way, complement has a broader manifesting set than object. Furthermore, while object is optional (although nuclear) in its clause type, complement is obligatory to its clause type. Finally, the two types of clause typically are ordered in contrasting sequence with the predicate first in the transitive clause and second in the equative clause. Thus, the Trique clause *da³ga³wi³⁵ʔ zi²¹ dq³h ngo⁴ tro²* 'That man killed a bull' (*da³ga³wi³⁵ʔ* 'killed', *zi²¹ dq³h* 'that man', *ngo⁴ tro²* 'a bull') is a transitive predication clause. But, *yq³⁴ n·e² re⁵ʔ w·į³ ri³ki³ kīhī³* 'where you live is in the forest' (*yq³⁴ n·e² re⁵ʔ* 'where live you', *w·į³* 'is'. *ri³ki³ kīhī³* 'in the forest') is an equative clause. As such, its subject 'where you live (subordinate clause) and its complement 'in the forest' (relator-axis phrase) are sequences which do not manifest actor and object of the transitive (or intransitive) predication clause.

In K'ekchi' there is a distinction between semi-transitive and transitive clause; yet both have similar structures:

$$\text{Semi-tr. Cl.: } (+P_{st} \pm S \pm O)$$
$$\text{Tr. Cl.: } \quad (+P_t \pm A \pm G)$$

Note the contrasting structure of the verbs manifesting the two predicates as sketched above in 1.2. Furthermore, O (object) and G (goal) contrast as well. As also noted in 1.2., clause level goal tagmeme is mutually exclusive with word level goal tagmeme, one or the other of which must occur in any given transitive clause. Object tagmeme may occur in a semi-transitive clause but is rare; furthermore when object tagmeme occurs it may not be manifested by a noun phrase beginning with the definite article *li*. Furthermore, it can be argued that the subject of the semi-transitive predicate is distinct from the actor of the transitive predicate in that the former cross-references to pronominal series A of verb prefixes while the latter cross-references to pronominal series B of verb prefixes. Semi-transitive clause: *ninkwaʔak kwa* 'I'm eating tortillas' (*n-* 'present tense, continuous action', *in-* 'I' of pronoun series A, *kwaʔak* 'to eat'). Transitive clause: *škwil li hasmin* 'I saw the jasmine' (*š-* 'past tense, completed action', *kw-* 'I' of pronoun series B, *-il* verb stem 'to see', *li hasmin* 'the jasmine').

In Ixil besides transitive and intransitive clause types distinguished on the basis of criteria of the sort already described, there is a further semi-transitive clause type. Both the intransitive and the semi-transitive clauses have two nuclear and obligatory clause level tagmemes:

$$\text{Intr.:} \quad +P_1 +S$$
$$\text{Semi-tr.:} +Ag +P_3$$

P_1 and P_3 symbolize two predicate tagmemes distinguished structurally by presence of a suffix *-on* 'passive' within P_3. S (subject) and Ag (agent) may be manifested by noun expressions, but the pronominal series manifesting agent is not entirely identical with the series of pronominal post-clitics manifesting subject. More distinctive, however, than the slight difference in pronouns manifesting agent versus subject is the fact that while subject never precedes P_1, agent always precedes P_3. Thus, tagmemes that are similar across the two clause types are distinguished from each other by differences of internal structure (presence versus absence of suffix *-on* 'passive' in P_3 versus P_1) and by differences of mutual ordering in each clause plus a more tenuous difference of manifesting class (subject following P_1, versus agent preceding P_3 plus slight differences in pronouns manifesting subject versus agent). While *kat ul i stoh* 'he came afoot' (*kat ul* 'came, *i* 'he', *stoh* 'afoot') is an Ixil intransitive clause, *ak kat banon* 'it was done by him' (*ak* 'he', *kat banon* 'was done') is a semi-transitive clause displaying the features just listed.

The English active (transitive) clause and passive clause each contains three nuclear tagmemes:

$$\text{Act. Tr. Cl.: } +S +P_a \pm O$$
$$\text{Pass. Cl.: } \quad +S +P_p \pm Ag$$

These two clause types differ as to predicate tagmemes (active versus passive predicates) and as to occurrence of object in the active clause versus agent in the passive clause (noun phrase preceded by *by*).

The Zoque intransitive subordinate clause described under 2.3. can be contrasted with the intransitive interrogative clause as follows:

$$\text{Intr. Sub.: } \pm sb +P_{1s} \pm S$$
$$\text{Intr. Inter.: } +Int +P_1 \pm S$$

Here, the subordinator tagmeme manifested by subordinate conjunctions contrasts with the interrogative tagmeme. The latter is manifested by about a dozen words, each of which substitutes for and is mututally exclusive with the manifestation of a given clause level tagmeme. Thus *ʔiyʌ* 'who' will occur rather than a clause level subject and *huhčʌk* 'when' rather than a clause level temporal. A second structural difference is seen in the contrast of P_{1s} (subordinate predicate) optionally marked with a suffix and P_1 (intransitive predicate).

2.5. Separate as different clause types any two varieties which have the same number of nuclear tagmemes provided that (a) one nuclear tagmeme of the one contrasts with a nuclear tagmeme of the other and (b) a second difference can be found. This contingency is presumably rare in that any second contrast diagnostic of separate clause types usually emerges as nuclear – in which case 2.4. is applicable. Possibly, however, the contrast between Hebrew intransitive active clause and nominal (equative) clause is illustrative:

$$\text{Intr. Cl.:} \quad +P_1 \pm S$$
$$\text{Nom. Cl.:} \quad +P_n +S$$

Clearly here an intransitive predicate such as *ḳum* '(he) arose' is distinct from such a nominal predicate as *ṣur* 'rock'. But either may have as subject the same type of substantive expression (e.g., *Ɂlohim* 'God' in such clauses as *ḳum Ɂlohim* 'God arose' and *ṣur Ɂlohim* 'God (is) a rock'). Nevertheless, while clause level subject is optional in the Hebrew intransitive clause it is obligatory in the nominal clause. (But here again, this optional-obligatory difference could lead to positing a tagmemic distinction between the subject of an intransitive verb and the subject found in a nominal clause – in which case the example falls under 2.4.)

2.6. Set up a distinct relator-axis (subordinate) clause type if one or more such types have not been already posited according to procedures 2.2.-2.5. above.

This separate procedure is framed to detect a further clause type whose distinguishing features are: (a) addition of a preposed subordinator; and (b) distinctive immediate constituent layering (cf. 1.0.). Thus, Trique subordinate clauses differ from independent clauses in that a subordinator such as nga^{43} 'when', nda^{43} 'until', or yq^{34} 'where' is present. Such a subordinator may be preposed to a transitive predication clause, an intransitive predication clause, an equative clause, or a meteorological clause (subjectless clauses such as 'raining', 'night falls', 'dawns'). Have we, then, subordinate and independent types corresponding to the fourfold distinction above and yielding a total of eight types of Trique? While such an analysis seems to be clearly warranted for Zoque (cf. 2.8.) and is congenial to the matrix approach to clause types as summarized in 2.8. and 2.9., nevertheless it does not seem warranted for Trique. A pair of clause types thus posited for Trique – say, independent and dependent meteorological ('raining' versus 'when raining') – would be separated by but one structural difference, viz. absence versus presence of subordinator. We posit, therefore, not four contrasting types of subordinate clause but rather one type consisting of +relator +axis – and note that axis may be manifested by any one of the first four Trique clause types. That clause types thus nest within clause types is no stranger than that phrase types nest within phrase types (e.g., noun phrase types in prepositional phrases).

2.7. Join any two varieties of clauses not separated by a dual structural contrast (or distinguished only by lexical co-occurrence restrictions) into one clause type with etic variants – unless strong analogical pressures require a separation.

Every structurally distinct manifestation of a given clause level tagmeme determines an etic variety of that clause type. Thus, etic varieties of the same clause are determined by the various verb phrase types which may manifest its predicate tagmeme or the various noun phrase types that may manifest its actor – to name but two points of variation. Likewise, etic variants are determined by presence or absence of a given optional tagmeme.

Lexical co-occurrence restrictions affecting open classes can be illustrated by mutual selections of verb and object in many languages. Undoubtedly, e.g., the English noun objects that occur with a transitive verb such as *slice* are different from the nouns that occur with *sweep* but perhaps not so different from those occurring with *eat* and even less different from those occurring with *cut*.

Lexical co-occurrence restrictions involving closed classes may also occur. Why, for example, do we not consider the following clauses to be different in English?

(a) *Empty carts make the most noise.*

(b) *An empty cart makes the most noise.*

In clauses such as (a) plural nouns occur while in (b) singular nouns occur. In (a) the verb in third person present tense is plural; in (b) the verb is marked as singular by virtue of the *-s* ending. Does not this constitute a two-fold difference between these two varieties of clause? Note, however, that (1) with most English nouns 'singular' versus 'plural' is an obligatory category. It seems realistic to argue that not only plural is indicated but singular as well – although the latter is indicated by a zero feature. (2) For this reason, we set up an obligatory number tagmeme occurring with all nouns (except mass nouns and *deer, sheep, trout* etc.) and having an overt manifestation (plural morpheme) and a covert manifestation (unmarked singular). For third person present verbs we set up another number tagmeme with overt manifestation (singular morpheme) and covert manifestation (unmarked plural). (3) It now appears that the putative difference between the two varieties of clause is simply a co-occurrence feature between the particular manifestations of two tagmemes:

Number tagmeme of subject	Number tagmeme of 3d present predicate
singular (covert)	singular (overt)
plural (overt)	plural (covert)

Occasionally, strong analogical pressures may result in positing a distinction on the basis of only one structural difference between two varieties of clause. This is procedurally the grammatical counterpart of positing a phonemic distinction on the basis of analogical pressures even in the absence of well-delineated contrast. Thus, in a given language there may be clear contrast between /p/ and /b/, /t/ and /d/, /k/ and /g/, and /kʷ/ and /gʷ/, but only poorly-delineated contrast between /ḍ/ and /ṭ/. In such circumstances analogy would surely lead us to posit the latter distinction as well (nor is such a judgment considered to invalidate the general insistence that phones accorded phonemic status must be in contrast). Similarly, there is in Zoque clause structure a clear contrast between indicative and subordinate clauses. As seen under 2.4. above, a Zoque subordinate clause has subordinating conjunction and/or subordinating suffix on the predicate. It is the possibility of both features which distinguishes the subordinate clause type. Nevertheless, of the six subtypes of subordinate clause in Zoque (manner, location, time, cause, purpose, participial) there is one sub-type, cause, which is introduced by subordinating conjunction but is not characterized by subordinating affix on the predicate. Here the analogy of the other five sub-types of subordinate clause leads us to consider cause clauses also to be subordinate clauses in contrast to the indicative, interrogative, and imperative – in spite of the fact that a two-fold difference does not characterize cause clauses. Nor does such a decision invalidate the general insistence on more than one difference in separating types.

2.8. Arrange partially similar but systematically contrasting clause types in one or more matrices with appropriate dimensions.

Thus Zoque clause types may be arranged in a matrix as follows:

	Indicative	Subordinate	Interrogative	Imperative
Intransitive	X	X	X	X
Transitive	X	X	X	X
Ditransitive	X	X	X	X
Descriptive	X	X	X	

In that the descriptive series has no clause type of the imperative order only fifteen types occur in this four by four matrix. A composite formula may be given for all indicative clause types: $+$(Nuc) $\pm$Peri ($\pm$IA $\pm$BP^n $\pm$M^2 $\pm$L^2 $\pm$T^2 $\pm$C) in which Nuc = nucleus, Peri = periphery, IA = instrumental-accompaniment, BP = benefactive-purpose, M = manner, L = locational, T = temporal, and C = cause. Superscript ^{n} = may occur an indefinite number of times in a given clause. Superscript ^{2} = may occur twice in a given clause.

Within the indicative order, the four clause types (intransitive, transitive, ditransitive, and descriptive) differ as to nuclei characteristic of each, plus a restriction of the periphery in the descriptive clause (IA does not occur). Each clause type in the indicative order may be transformed to a subordinate, interrogative, or imperative clause type (minus descriptive imperative) by simple tranform rules.

2.9. Inspect the posited matrix or matrices for (a) confirmation of types, and (b) clues as to possible types yet uncatalogued.

Thus, examination of the Zoque matrix just given seems to confirm the types posited – some of which were found after a preliminary matrix of the same general shape was found to contain lacunae. The non-occurrence of descriptive imperative remains, however, as a genuine lacuna. Sporadic documentation of rare clauses containing more than two objects suggests the possibility that four more clause types should be posited, i.e. polytransitive indicative, subordinate, interrogative, and imperative.

3. ANALYTICAL PROCEDURES FOR CLAUSE LEVEL TAGMEMES

3.0.1. Prepare an exhaustive list of the items or sequences manifesting each clause level tagma in each clause type whenever the set which manifests a tagma is not readily summarizable.

In K'ekchi', one would scarcely find it necessary to list the items manifesting predicate$_1$ tagma of the semi-transitive clause or the items manifesting predicate$_2$ tagma of the transitive clause in that both are manifested by syntagmemes (semi-transitive verb construction versus transitive verb construction) that are readily identifiable as distinct morphological structures. But for K'ekchi' it is well to list the items and sequences manifesting every other clause level tagma. If each such summary list of items and sequences manifesting a clause level tagma can be put upon a single page (or at most only two or three pages) it will considerably facilitate scanning of the lists.

3.0.2. Attempt to summarize in statement form the items and sequences manifesting each tagma. The purpose of this summary statement is to make explicit for tagmemic analysis considerations often so abstruse as not to be in focus unless some step of this sort is taken. This summary statement will probably not be couched in terms which the analyst would want to use in a grammar write-up to be sent to the editor of a professional journal, but will to some degree reflect crude labels and mnemonic devices of practical value only to the analyst himself at this stage of his work.

For locational tagma in Trique such a tentative summary would read: "Nouns of place (including names of towns, localities, public buildings, and words like 'lake', 'bathhouse', 'canyon'). Nouns of person (cf. 'indirect object' in some languages). Item-possessor noun phrases (body parts). Relator-axis phrases. Clauses introduced by yq^{34} 'place where', $ne^{34}P$ 'over towards', nda^{43} yq^{34} 'as far as the place where'."

Notice that in the above summary statement for locational tagma reference is made to several phrase types, and to a word class (noun). This underscores again the practical impossibility of analyzing any one structural level such as clause structure in complete isolation from other levels. Actually some of the more salient facts about word and phrase structure either should be understood before beginning clause analysis or need to be analyzed at least in preliminary fashion while performing such analysis. The Trique relator-axis phrase, which is restricted to three peripheral tagmemes in the Trique predication clause, was discovered and catalogued as a phrase type during the analysis of Trique clause structure. For a discussion of emic word classes see the introduction.

3.0.3. In performing these listing and summarizing procedures the analyst may discover inconsistencies in his early impressionistic identification of clause level tagmas. Thus an item may have been charted in one column which on further analysis more probably belongs in another column. In the analysis of Trique clause structure occasional reassignment of an item from the object column to the locational or *vice versa* was necessary.

3.1. List as tagmemically separate the tagmas that without further analysis already appear to be unequivocably distinct from each other on distributional-semantic grounds. For example, within a given clause type in a given language, such nuclear tagmemes as predicate tagma, actor tagma, and object may appear as unequivocably distinct on the basis of: (a) distinctive physical positions; (b) difference in obligatory versus optional status; (c) distinctive manifestations in terms of word classes; (d) distinctive manifestations in terms of word types, phrase types, or subordinate clauses; (e) distinctive cross reference of certain nuclear tagmemes to affixes within the verb manifesting predicate; (f) distinctive transforms.

3.2. Look for pairs of tagmas that are suspect of being the same tagmeme in that they exhibit similarities in respect to one or more of the following considerations: manifesting class, internal structure (whether word or phrase), slot meaning, and position(s) of occurrence. Some typical pairs of suspect tagmas are: object/locational-directional, locational-directional/positional, locational/manner, locational/locational-in-logical-space, locational/time, locational/benefactive, time/manner, object/indirect object, object/second object, indirect object/benefactive, indirect object/reference, cause/agent, cause/instrument, agent/instrument. If tagmas have been labeled according to manifesting particles and classes as suggested in 1.2. − pairs of tagmas may be considered suspect if they exhibit formal similarities. In Hebrew various tagmas introduced by *l-* 'to/for' and *ʔel* 'to' would be considered mutually suspect (see 3.3. below), while *l-* + noun meaning 'to/for someone' would be treated as suspect with *l-* + noun meaning 'as an x' or 'in the role of an x' and also with *l-* + noun (temporal) meaning 'at so-and-so time'. The analyst should especially consider as suspect any two tagmas which caused a practical difficulty in procedure 1.5. in respect to inconsistent charting of similar or identical items in first one column then in the other, or tagmas which caused difficulty in procedure 3.0.2. so that it proved difficult to summarize in statement form the items and sequences manifesting one tagma versus those manifesting another (although, of course, two tagmemes may have identical manifesting sets if other features such as word order or cross reference distinguish them functionally).

3.3. Join as one tagmeme any two tagmas which are similar as indicated above, which occur in the same clause type, and which are in noncontrastive distribution (i.e., free variation and/or complementary distribution). Thus, in Biblical Hebrew there occur two constructions *Pel* 'to' +pronoun and *l-* 'to/for' + pronoun both of which mean 'to/for someone' and both of which occur with high statistical frequency between verb and subject when the latter two occur in this order in Hebrew narrative prose. There also occurs with high statistical frequency the same general sort of construction – in this case *Pel* or *l-* + noun (personal) – in two possible orderings out beyond the subject (when verb and subject occur in this order). There is a strong tendency for the two tagmas (one involving pronouns and in pre-subject slot; the other involving nouns and in one of two post-subject slots) to be in noncontrastive distribution; they may be considered to constitute an indirect object or benefactive-referent tagmeme in Biblical Hebrew.

In K'ekchi' there occur five tagmas manifesting a spectrum of meaning ranging from 'cause' to 'agent' to 'instrument' to 'accompaniment' and to 'lack of accompaniment'. Five particles accompanied by pronoun prefixes plus or minus a following epexegetical noun expression occur manifesting these five tagmas: *-ban* 'by', *-mak* 'because', *-ikPin* 'with', *-očben* 'in the company of', *-hunes* 'alone'. But the range of meaning of each particle in reference to the range of meaning of all five tagmas can best be seen in chart form as below (where the horizontal axis represents types of observed meaning and the vertical axis represents the particles; the meanings of the particles are given at the intersection of the axes):

	Agent	Cause	Instrument	Accompaniment	Lack of Accompaniment
-ban	X	X	X		
-mak		X			
ikPin		X	X	X	
-očben				X	
-hunes					X

The chart shows that while *-mak* 'because', *-očben* 'in the company of' and *-hunes* 'alone' are fairly discrete as to meaning, nevertheless *-ban* 'by' overlaps in three semantic areas (1-3) and *-ikPin* 'with' overlaps in three semantic areas (2-4). Any attempt to posit, say, an agent-cause-instrument tagmeme (manifested by phrases involving the first three particles) versus an accompaniment-lack-of-accompaniment tagmeme (manifested by the last two particles) is baffled by the failure of the five distinguishable meanings to correspond neatly to the five morphemes involved. Furthermore, the five tagmas as a group can be distinguished from other K'ekchi' tagmemes (benefactive, time, location, purpose) which have different manifesting classes and/or structurally distinguishable manifesting sequences. We assume, therefore, that these five tagmas constitute one K'ekchi' tagmeme which, for want of a better name, has been termed 'cause'.

3.4. Separate tagmemically any two suspect tagmas that may occur together in the same clause provided that there is some semantically significant difference in the mutual ordering of the two tagmas, in manifesting set, or in possible transforms.

Order will probably prove to be but one of several identifying-contrastive features characteristic of the one tagmeme as opposed to the other. Order may, however, constitute the crucial distinguishing feature between two tagmemes in a given language whenever an exceptionless distributional statement can be made concerning the mutual ordering of the two. Thus, in Hebrew there are two suspect tagmas *l-* + noun/pronoun meaning 'to someone' or 'for someone' and *l-* + noun, meaning 'as an x', 'in the role of an x.' These two tagmas may occur in sequence in the same clause where the 'to' or 'for' expression invariably precedes the 'in the role of' expression. In Genesis 23:20: *wayyɔqɔm haśśɔdɛ whamm'ɔrɔ Pšɛr-bo lPɔbrɔham lPḥuzzat-qɔber* ... 'and-it-was-made-sure the-field and-the-cave which-(was)-in-it to-Abraham as-a-possession-of-burial', the phrase 'to-Abraham' (*lPɔbrɔham*) precedes the phrase 'as-a-possession-of-burial' (*lPḥuzzat-qɔber*). This ordering feature along with the fact that the noun following *l-* 'to/for' is restricted to personal noun while the noun following *l-* 'in the role of' is not so restricted identifies the former as manifesting an indirect object tagmeme versus the latter which manifests role tagmeme.

In Trique, locational tagmeme is distinguishable from object tagmeme by several identifying-contrastive features among which is the fact that while object comes regularly in second orbit out fro m the predicate, locational with high statistical frequency is limited to orbits further out.

A clear distinction in the items and sequences that manifest two tagmas occurring in the same clause is often a very crucial identifying-contrastive feature. Thus in Ixil a benefactive tagmeme is distinguished from a locational tagmeme in that while the latter may be manifested by a noun of relatively unrestricted class preceded by a complex consisting of pronoun plus one of several particles meaning 'location at or in', 'environment-of' (including 'accompaniment'), and 'location relative to', the former is limited to nouns referring to person or animal preceded by a complex consisting of pronoun plus the particle *-e* 'direction' or 'reference'. There is, furthermore, a corroborative consideration of ordering, i.e. only with great rarity does benefactive as thus defined not precede locational. Note the following analyzed Ixil clause *kat yolon in te nah tu koʔm* 'I spoke to the man in the cornfield' where *te nah* 'to the man' (*t-e* 'his direction', *nah* 'man') manifests benefactive and *tu koʔm* 'in the cornfield' (*t-u* 'its in-ness', *koʔm* 'cornfield') manifests locational.

If the two suspect tagmas occurring in the same clause transform differently they should be regarded as tagmemically distinct. Thus in such a Latin sentence as *sui eum regem apellant* 'they call him king', *eum* 'him' is direct object, while *regem* 'king' (also accusative case) manifests a suspect tagma which could be considered to be a repeat occurrence of direct object tagmeme or a further tagmeme. That the latter is true is seen in that in transforming to passive voice *eum* 'him' becomes *is* 'he' subject, while *regem* 'king' becomes *rex* 'king' which is now predicate nominative: *is rex ab suis appelatur* 'he is called king by his subjects'.

3.5. Consider that a repeat sequence of the same tagmeme is constituted by two (or more) suspect tagmas that occur in continuous or discontinuous sequence in the same clause without semantically significant difference in order, in manifesting set, or in possible transforms.

It is by no means unusual to find one or more tagmemes occurring in repeat sequences in a given language. (If such a sequence is continuous, however, and formally linked by some sort of conjunction it is better to consider the whole a phrase of coordinate structure, e.g., cf. Hebrew coordinate positional phrase in Genesis 24:29: *ʿal yɔmin ʔo ʿal śmol* 'to (the) right or to (the) left'.)

In Hebrew repeat sequences of positional tagmeme (manifested by prepositional phrases) as well as repeat sequences of temporal tagmeme (manifested by a temporal noun plus or minus preceding *l-* 'at') are by no means uncommon; the fact that these tagmemes frequently occur in repeat sequence could be considered to constitute a further identifying contrastive feature of them. In the following example (Genesis 24:11) there is a repeat sequence of positional followed by a repeat sequence of temporal: *wayyabrek₁ haggmɔllim₂ miḥus lɔʿir₃ ʔɛl bʔer hammɔyim₄ lʿet ʿereb₅ lʔet ṣet haśśoʔbot₆*. 'He-caused-to-kneel₁ the-camels₂ at-the-outside-of-the-city₃ at well-of water₄ at-hour-of-evening₅ at-hour-of going-forth-of the-(women)-drawing (water)₆'. In the above *miḥus lɔʿir* 'at-the-outside-of the-city' and *ʔɛl bʔer hammɔyim* 'at well-of water' constitute a repeat sequence of positional tagmeme while *lʿet ʿereb* 'at-the-hour-of evening' and *lʿet ṣet haśśoʔbot* 'at-the-hour-of going-forth-of the-(women)-drawing (water)' constitute a repeat sequence of temporal tagmeme.

Repeat sequences of this sort involving especially such tagmemes as locational, time, and benefactive have been observed in several Mayan languages. E.g., in Aguacatec repeat sequences of benefeactive (or indirect object) involving up to four juxtaposed phrases have been observed.

In Trique occurrences of two locationals or of two temporal modifiers in the same clause are not uncommon. In such circumstances one occurrence of the tagmeme is usually clause initial while the other is clause final (with the longer and more involved construction more likely to occur in the latter position).

In the composite formula (2.8.) for Zoque indicative clause, manner, locational, and temporal each are indicated as capable of occurring twice in the same clause, while benefactive-purpose is indicated as capable of occurring an indefinite number of times.

3.6. Separate any two suspect tagmas which occur in different clause types and are in any way formally distinct.

Thus, as stated in 2.3., the subject of a Zoque intransitive clause is tagmemically distinct from the actor of a Zoque transitive clause in that nouns manifesting actor have a case marking suffix $-\textit{Ps} \sim -\textit{Pis}$.

Similarly (2.4.), the object of a K'ekchi' semi-transitive clause is tagmemically distinct from the goal of a K'ekchi' transitive clause in that noun phrases manifesting goal may begin with the definite article *li* while noun phrases manifesting object may not.

3.7. Look for sequences of tagmas that are suspect of being not two distinct clause level tagmemes, but only one long manifestation of a single clause level tagmeme, in that the sequence seems to occur en bloque regardless of how a clause may pattern as to word order. This is essentially a matter of determining how many tagmemic cuts to make on the clause level versus the phrase level in a given language. Thus, there occurs in Trique a small class of modifiers of which ru^3wa^{23} 'almost', and a^5P 'already' are typical. This class of items is found immediately preceding the verb in a Trique clause without any intervening elements. In such circumstances the decision must be made as to whether a suspect sequence such as ru^3wa^{23} 'almost' + verb is to be considered to manifest one clause level tagmeme (with internal tagmemic distinctions on the phrase level) or two clause level tagmemes – thus setting up a new clause level tagmeme not previously posited for Trique, i.e. some sort of manner tagmeme.

A similar problem in Trique has to do with specific lexical collocations of certain verbs and certain nouns in a construction in which the noun apparently patterns as an object which occurs in an otherwise anomalous position between predicate and actor. For example, while such examples as gi^3Pya^3h zi^3 $go^3no^3Po^2$ 'made he medicine' reflect a very common ordering (predicate, actor, object) the particular verb gi^3Pya^3h 'made' and the particular noun $go^3no^3Po^2$ 'medicine' also occur in what appears to be a statistically rare ordering (predicate, object, actor) in such a example as gi^3Pya^3h $go^3no^3Po^2 zi^3$ 'made medicine he'. In this circumstance, however, we treat gi^3Pya^3h $go^3no^3Po^2$ 'made medicine' as a sequence suspect of manifesting but one clause level tagmeme (predicate) but characterized by internal tagmemic distinction on the phrase level (i.e. with some sort of phrase level incorporated object tagmeme).

3.8. Join a suspect sequence of tagmas into one clause level tagmeme whenever overall tactical considerations make it simpler to posit further complications on a lower level (phrase or word) rather than on the clause level itself. As a secondary criterion it is often useful to note whether the set manifesting one of the two tagmas in question is of small and restricted or large and open membership, in that an aberrant pattern on the clause level constituted by occurrence of a few items in an unusual position is likely to prove to be a feature of some lower level structure rather than of clause structure proper.

In regard to the Trique problem of whether to consider ru^3wa^{23} 'almost' + verb as manifesting two clause level tagmemes or as one clause level tagmeme, there are certain overall tactical considerations that point decisively towards the latter. To posit a clause level manner tagmeme would complicate our statement of Trique clause structure in that it would now be necessary to qualify the statement that "Actor always appears in first orbit to the predicate" with the proviso: "except when manner tagmeme intervenes and displaces actor to second orbit". On the other hand phrase structure of considerable complexity occurs in Trique and it is no great complication to add another peripheral phrase level tagmeme to the general structure of verb phrases. Furthermore, note that the set of items manifesting this manner tagmeme is of quite small and restricted membership – a consideration which seems relevant to Trique where tagmemes of restricted manifestation occur typically on the phrase and word levels rather than the clause level.

Our second Trique suspect sequence above, that composed of particular lexical collocations of verbs and nouns in a pattern that apparently gives an anomalous order predicate, object, actor, may similarly be decided in favor of one clause level tagmeme with further complexity relegated to the phrase level. Thus, while $gi^3ʔya^3h$ zi^3 $go^3no^3ʔo^2$ 'made he medicine' is assumed to manifest three clause level tagmemes (predicate, actor, object), the rarer ordering $gi^3ʔya^3h$ $go^3no^3ʔo^2$ zi^3 'made medicine he' is assumed to manifest but two clause level tagmemes (predicate manifested by $gi^3ʔya^3h$ $go^3no^3ʔo^2$ 'made medicine' and actor manifested by zi^3 'he'. Again there is here the tactical consideration of preserving, if possible, our statement that "Actor always appears in first orbit to the predicate" – since the latter holds true for the great mass of our data and seems, in fact, to constitute one of the identifying-contrastive features of actor as opposed to object. Positing of an incorporated object tagmeme on the (verb) phrase level adds a complication, to be sure, at that level; but, again, it is well to recall that the phrase level typically is complicated in Trique and another complication need not surprise us (there are some 25 syntagmemically distinct phrase types in Trique with some sixty constituent tagmemes). Furthermore, our second criterion above is also relevant in that the nouns occurring as incorporated objects constitute a small group each of which pairs off with a particular verb in what appear to be very specialized, derivative-like patterns.

On the other hand although actor tagma always occurs en bloque with predicate tagma within the Trique clause we would scarcely want to join actor and predicate into one clause level tagmeme on this basis. Overall tactical considerations do not make it simpler to join actor and predicate tagmemes into one clause level tagmeme in that a very new sort of phrase formation – one involving predication – would be posited along with an internal complexity of phrase structure by far exceeding that of any other phrase type yet posited. Furthermore, both predicate and actor in Trique are tagmemes characterized by the most varied and extensive manifesting sets of any tagmemes in the language, so that the manifestation of the predicate tagmemes of various clause types is for all practical purposes coextensive with verb while the manifestation of actor tagmeme includes the majority of items called nouns. In terms of both our first and second criteria a sequence of predicate and actor – which is, as a matter of fact, scarcely worth considering to be a suspect sequence at all – can not be interpreted as manifesting but one clause level tagmeme.

4. CONCLUDING PROCEDURES FOR CLAUSE LEVEL ANALYSIS (SUMMARY, EXPANSION, AND CROSS-CHECKING)

4.1. If in the course of the above analysis the various items in the residue column of the chart set up according to procedure 1.4. have not been analyzed tagmemically, then these residues should be reexamined so that either (a) each residue is assigned to a tagmeme now identified by the above procedures, or (b) certain residues are assigned to a clause level tagmeme not previously posited. If (b) prove true, then this new tagmeme should be examined as to position(s) of occurrence, manifesting set, and slot meaning.

In Trique, instrumental tagmeme was thus isolated by studying residues. Also a few items wrongly classed as objects were seen to be instrumentals once this further tagmeme was posited.

4.2. Write a brief summary sketch of the clause level syntagmemes and tagmemes of the language. For each syntagmeme (clause type) indicate whatever identifying-contrastive features distinguish one clause type versus the other (see section 2). This requires that minimal-maximal formulae be given for each clause type along with mention of any transforms that prove to be syntagmemically relevant, as well as any features of concord within the clause types. For each clause level tagmeme indicate position(s) of occurrence (almost entirely free in some languages, very restricted in others), slot meaning, the set of manifesting items – in terms of classes of words and/or morphemes; in terms of occurring phrase structures or of subordinate clauses; and in terms of overt markers identifying the item or sequence manifesting one tagmeme as opposed to another. The latter is illustrated by Latin or Greek case endings or by particles indicative of syntactic function in Malayo-Polynesian.

The analyst need not be unduly disturbed if he has difficulty thinking up appropriate name-labels to distinguish one tagmeme or syntagmeme from another. He should search for a label that is as adequate as he can find in respect to the slot meaning of each tagmeme that he catalogues, but should remember that his name-labels are but name-labels and will ultimately receive meaning only by virtue of usage in the grammatical description that he is producing. In this respect grammar fares neither better nor worse than any other taxonomic science. In calling a clause level K'ekchi' tagmeme 'cause' when the full meaning of the tagmeme includes not merely 'cause' but 'agent', 'instrument', 'accompaniment', and 'lack of accompaniment' as well, we are no worse off than in zoology where *Megachiroptera* include certain small bats, *Microchiroptera* include certain large bats, and *Carnivora* include a few pure vegetarians like the giant panda.

4.3. Check rapidly the above description of clause structure against a larger corpus. Look out for data that adds to, clarifies, or modifies the description. Disregard data of the sort already catalogued and analyzed unless one finds a particularly apt example of some point not too well exemplified previously.

My original pilot study of Biblical Hebrew (based on but four chapters of Genesis) gave an interesting sketch of the Hebrew verb clause. Subsequent checking through most of Genesis and half of Exodus has resulted, however, in certain clarifications and modifications. A few points where the broader corpus modifies the former sketch are: (1) *l-/ʔɛl* 'to/for' + noun (indirect object) was considered in its outermost position (beyond the object when present in the order: predicate, subject, object) to be positionally indeterminate with *l-* 'in the role of' + noun (role). Subsequent data reveals that the latter invariably follows the former when both occur in the same clause. (2) Temporal noun had been charted just preceding positional; and *l-* 'at' + temporal noun had been charted just following positional. Further data have shown that either manifestation of temporal tagmeme may occur in either position, and have thus corroborated joining of these two tagmas into one tagmeme. (3) In the smaller corpus *l-* 'to/for' + pronoun and *ʔɛl* 'to' + pronoun (both manifesting indirect object) occurred only between predicate and subject when both these clause level tagmemes were present while the same two prepositional elements followed by a noun (also manifesting indirect object) occurred only out beyond the subject when both predicate and subject were present in that order. There was, therefore, a watertight scheme of complementary distribution involving the two tagmas. Further study has revealed, however, that there are exceptions to this scheme so that while the above statements are valid with high statistical probability (and, therefore, by no means structurally irrelevant) they are no longer exceptionless. (4) A few other prepositions besides *l-* and *Pɛl* were found to introduce the indirect object tagmeme.

4.4. Revise description to account for the fuller corpus and write up the clause structure in more complete form. Proceed as indicated in 4.2. with special care to add enough examples to make the paper genuinely useful to someone else. Be sure to analyze every example so that the reader can follow it. Be doubly sure that every symbol is explained as first introduced.

II

PHRASE LEVEL PROCEDURES

5. PRELIMINARY PROCEDURES FOR PHRASE LEVEL ANALYSIS

5.0. Definition of phrase: a class of syntagmemes of a hier-archical order ranking above such syntagmemes as the word and/or stem and below such syntagmemes as the clause and sentence. It may be single-centered, double-centered, or relator-axis; and ex-presses such relationships as head-modifier, linkage of elements, or relation of an element to the clause by means of an overt relator (e.g., English prepositional phrases).

While the phrase constitutes a lower hierarchical level than the clause, it ranks higher than the word and/or stem. In the English phrase *the slow, lumbering, covered wagon* the two word units, *lumbering* and *covered* have internal structures of their own appro-priate to their structural level. In Zoque, there is not only a phrase level, but two clearly distinct levels below the phrase, viz. word and stem. The former involves stem-affix strings which may be described in terms of relative orders of affixes; the latter involves strings which must be described in terms of various layered derivational patterns involving both root compounding and affixation. Cashibo exem-plifies a more involved situation in which (presumably) rudimentary phrase structures comprise a level ranking above three lower struc-tural levels, viz. word, base, and core (plus root which is by defini-tion not expandable on its own level and therefore not a syntag-meme). Most Mayan languages exemplify a situation in which a common undifferentiated word-phrase level (including inflectional elements) ranks above a derivational (stem) level.

In that phrases may be single-centered (*the great black shambling bear*), double-centered (*John and Mary*), or relator-axis (*to the store*) they show considerable variety of internal structure. In single-centered phrases some sort of HEAD or MAIN element occurs along with one or more MODIFYING, ATTRIBUTIVE, or QUALIFYING elements. In double-centered phrases two members of equal rank (and typically of identical structure) occur with or without an OVERT LINK (conjunction). In relator-axis phrases the RELATOR is a preposition, a postposition, or a noun or particle in specialized function.

The phrase shows a corresponding variety of structural meaning which is not readily amenable to summary. Nevertheless, broadly conceived, three categories of meaning are implied by the structural classification just indicated: MODIFICATION, LINKAGE, and RELATION by means of an overt relator. Modification here is meant to cover phrases containing auxiliaries, adverbs, possessors, quantifiers, classifiers, attributives, identifiers, deictics, and similar elements. Linkage covers not only coordinate phrases but phrases expressing alternation (*two or three*, Trique *w·i^{5}h wa^{5}ʔni^{5}h* 'two or three' – without conjunction), mutual exclusion (*either Tom or Bill*) and mutual dependency (*both Tom and Mary*). Relation by means of an overt relator is exemplified by the phrase *to the store* in which *to* relates the phrase of which it is a part to the rest of the clause: *I went to the store.*

5.1. Isolate phrase units in the corpus being analyzed. Every sequence bounded by borders of clause level tagmemes is a phrase unless (a) it has an internal structure which requires us to consider it to be a syntagmeme on a higher level (e.g., an imbedded clause or sentence); or (b) it has an internal structure more characteristic of the word or stem levels than of the phrase level – and aside from this sort of structure figures in no sequences lower than the clause level itself; or (c) it is a root (which does not constitute a minimal phrase and hence occurs in no sequence lower than clause or sentence).

Thus, in the clause *the old oak table | had been polished | with great care | when I arrived*, vertical lines mark boundaries of clause level tagmemes. The sequences thus bounded are *the old oak table, had been polished, with great care*, and *when I arrived*. Of these sequences the first three are phrases. The fourth sequence, however, is not a phrase in that it has the internal structure of a clause.

A phrase need not be complex in every manifestation. Most languages have one or more phrase types with but one obligatory phrase level tagmeme. Thus, in the Trique clause ga^3ka^{34} $\check{z}u^3we^3$ 'the dog got burned', $\check{z}u^3we^3$ 'dog' manifests not only clause level actor tagmeme but phrase level head tagmeme as well. This latter function is more clearly seen in ga^3ka^{34} $\check{z}u^3we^3$ ga^5ci^5 dq^3h 'that white dog got burned' where $\check{z}u^3we^3$ ga^5ci^5 dq^3h 'that white dog' is an expansion of the head tagmeme by the addition of two words manifesting postposed optional tagmemes.

In Ixil there is a class of time particles which manifest clause level time tagmeme but which do not occur in sequences lower than the clause itself. These time particles (e.g. $\check{c}el$ 'today', $na\hat{P}ycan$ 'long ago', $o\check{s}i$ 'three days hence') do not manifest minimal phrase structures but are monomorphemic roots. Should one or more of these particles prove to consist of more than one morpheme the internal structure of the particle would be described on the stem level (as opposed to the undifferentiated word-phrase level in Ixil).

Phrases that usually occur bounded by borders of clause level tagmemes may on occasion be found imbedded within another phrase. Thus, while *John's brother* may occur manifesting clause level subject (and is thus bounded by borders of clause level tagmemes), it may also occur imbedded in the phrase *the career of John's brother*. Expansion of a phrase by the addition of further optional tagmemes possible in a phrase type (e.g. *black notebooks* versus *unobtrusive little black notebooks*) should be distinguished from imbedding of phrase type within phrase type (e.g. *a friend of the daughter of my first cousin Gertrude*). Criteria for distinguishing the latter are given in 5.6.

Phrase types which occur only imbedded in other phrase types may occur as well. Thus certain Trique numeral phrases occur only as manifestations of quantity tagmeme in the periphery of several types of noun phrases: $gq^5\hat{P}q^3h$ $\check{z}i^4a^4$ $\check{z}i^4nq^{45}\hat{P}$ $gq^5\hat{P}q^3h$ $ma^3c\Lambda h\Lambda^{43}$ 'ninety-nine sheep' in which $ma^3c\Lambda h\Lambda^{43}$ 'sheep' manifests head tagmeme of a noun phrase type while the preceding words ('four score fifteen four') are a numeral phrase which manifests quantity tagmeme within the framework of the noun phrase. This numeral phrase is in turn characterized by its own internal tagmemic structure.

5.2. Copy each phrase on a 3 × 5 or 4 × 6 filing slip with translation (if the latter is necessary for your handling of the data) and accurate reference to location in your corpus.

Some examples of minimal phrase structures should be filed, but a great quantity of phrases consisting of but one syntactic element does not contribute materially to the value of one's data while at the same time it contributes disproportionately to its bulk. Make a notation as to what clause level tagmeme is manifested by a given phrase. Distribution in the clause may be an important factor in distinguishing ambiguous examples once a classification is first made on the basis of the internal structure of the phrase itself. At least five hundred such phrases should be initially filed with subsequent addition of further phrases of whatever types prove to be inadequately represented.

5.3. Make a guess as to the number of separate charts that will handle the data well, and group the phrases accordingly. It may be expected that phrases with nouns as center (whether single-centered or double-centered) will differ structurally from phrases with verbs as center. In languages with no clear noun versus verb dichotomy on the word level it may nevertheless prove that phrases manifesting clause level predicate tagmemes differ from phrases manifesting various substantival functions (subject, object, indirect object, etc.). It is to be expected that single-centered noun phrases will be distinct from double-centered. Noun phrases expressing possession and apposition will very likely prove distinct from each other and from those involving a head with other sorts of modifiers. One or more types of relator-axis phrases can be expected. Temporal, locative, and manner phrases may prove to be distinct also. Adjective phrases, involving some device for intensifying or limiting an adjective are not uncommon, nor are combinations of particles into phrases which may be conjunctive, prepositional, or pronominal. Numeral phrases will be encountered – unless higher numerals prove to be word structures.

5.4. Make an etic identification of the tagmas within each phrase on each file slip by jotting over or under the line appropriate symbols or labels, such as head, attribute, quantifier, classifier, identifier, item, possessor, appositive, link, plural, main, auxiliary, intensifier, modifier, adverbial, aspect, mood, subject marker, object marker, locative marker, axis, related, multiplier, multiplied, numeral, increment, etc.

This procedure gives us phrase level tagmas, that is phrase segments which consist of function-set correlations tentatively identified as in 1.2. for clause above.

It is assumed that this procedure may be applied without focusing explicitly on the structure of lower levels such as the word. Here again, practical considerations of work programming prohibit our insisting that one attempt to analyze all levels simultaneously. The more, however, that one understands the structure of lower levels, the more valid will be the description of phrase structure. It is by no means rare to have a feature of word structure prove relevant on the phrase level. Illustrative of this is the marking of either possessed item or possessor in some morphological manner: Thus Trique preposes zi^3- to a possessed item as in zi^3-me^3sa^{23} '(someone's) table', while Hebrew has a characteristic internal stem change (resulting in a form called the 'construct state') for a possessed item so that *bet* 'house' is distinct from *bɛt* 'house-of' and *gmallim* 'camels' is distinct from *gmalle* 'camels-of'. English, in common with other Indo-European languages, inflects rather the possessor as in *boy's*.

5.5. When any group of phrases obtained by procedure 5.3. involves a sizable number of phrases (say more than 50) it is advantageous to file the slips in some fashion (similar to that suggested in 1.3.) so as to bring together at one spot all examples of phrases having the same center. The particular lexical selections of the items thus brought together can then be studied seriatim. Contrasting phrase types are often better seen in such circumstances with occasional uncovering of something roughly parallel with minimal contrast in phonology. For example, both of the following phrases would be filed under

Trique $\check{c}u^3h$ 'egg' (although probably in separate groups according to 5.3.): $\check{c}u^3h\ \check{z}u^3\check{c}e^{43}$ 'chicken egg' and $\check{z}i^3\check{c}u^{21}\ \check{z}u^3\check{c}e^{43}$ also translated 'chicken egg'. The latter phrase, in contrast to the first, contains a possessed stem $\check{z}i^3\check{c}u^{21}$ 'egg'. This leads one to suspect that the former construction consists of a head followed by an attributive (compare Trique $ga^3ga^3\mathcal{P}\ n.e\mathcal{P}e^3$ 'rope-like metal', i.e. 'wire' (ga^3-$ga\mathcal{P}a^3$ 'metal', $n\cdot e\mathcal{P}e^3$ 'rope')) while the latter is an item-possessor phrase.

More frequently, however, it will be found that certain nouns typically enter into a restricted number of phrase types. Thus, while ni^3ka^{34} 'mate-of, wife, husband' occurs necessarily as an item in an item-possessor phrase (i.e., is obligatorily possessed) and never manifests head of a qualifier-head phrase, $gwi^{35}\check{z}a^5na^{53}$ 'woman' occurs manifesting head and never manifesting item. These features emerge somewhat more readily with a filing technique of the sort here suggested.

With relator-axis phrases it may be useful to file according to word, particle, or affix manifesting relator tagma, although one could file according to the head word of the expression found in the axis slot.

5.6. Copy the data from the filing slips onto a series of charts with a separate chart for each group posited in 5.3. There should be a column for each phrase level tagma identified in 5.4. Here, as in clause structure, a residue column is needed. Columns are arranged in the statistically most common linear ordering of the tagmas – if such an ordering can be identified. Otherwise columns are arranged in an arbitrary order. Where, however, the order of columns does indicate a statistically common ordering of tagmas, departures from that order may be indicated by drawing arrows to indicate actually occurring orders. Where an arbitrary ordering of elements must be adopted small subscript numerals may be used to indicate the actual order. The latter expedient often leads to discovery of statistically-more-than-random orderings which were at first not suspected. For verb phrases in Trique a chart of the following sort might characterize this state of the analysis (the form of the chart varies somewhat according to the background and predilections of the analyst). In the following portion of such a chart, Trique verb phrases involving ga^3ni^{23} 'to stand up, to erect' are given:

Pre-V adv.	1st V slot	2nd V slot	Modifier	Repetitive	Metaphor-ical mod-ifier	Resi-due
		ga^3ni^{23}				
u^3ta^4 'much'		ga^3ni^{23}	$za^5\text{ʔ}$ 'well'			
$a^5\text{ʔ}$ 'already'		ga^3ni^{23}	ni^1ka^4 'straight'			
	$gq^3\text{ʔ}q^{34}h$ 'went'	ga^3ni^{23}				
	$ga^3\text{ʔ}na^{35}\text{ʔ}$ 'came'	ga^3ni^{23}				
ru^3wa^{23} 'about to'	$gq^4\text{ʔ}q^4h$	ga^4ni^4				
		ga^3ni^{23}	$za^5\text{ʔ}$			
$a^5\text{ʔ}$		ga^3ni^{23}				
		ga^3ni^{23}		yu^2 'again'		
		ga^3ni^{23}	$za^5\text{ʔ}$		ru^3wa^{23} 'inside'	
$a^5\text{ʔ}$		ga^3ni^{23}	$za^5\text{ʔ}$		ru^3wa^{23}	
	$gq^3\text{ʔ}q^{34}h$	ga^3ni^{23}	$za^5\text{ʔ}$		ru^3wa^{23}	

In charting of the sort here suggested several problems typically emerge. Two of these problems merit special attention: (1) The first problem involves charting a sequence of two words of the same broad class. It is assumed that two tagmemes are involved and that the class manifesting each tagmeme will need to be carefully delineated and described. But, when such an AB sequence occurs, do we file the whole construction under item A, under item B, or under both? Thus in the Trique data charted above, why is $gq^3\text{ʔ}q^{34}h$ ga^3ni^{23} 'went (and) erected (something)' filed under ga^3ni^{23} 'to erect' rather than under $gq^3\text{ʔ}q^{34}h$ 'to go'? Or, under what conditions should we file under both? Similarly, when we have two slots – such as 1st verb slot and 2nd verb slot in the above chart – in which slot do we place a given verb such as $ga^3n\check{i}^{23}$ 'erect' when it manifests a minimal verb phrase? Resolution of these problems requires attention to criteria for distinguishing internally COORDINATE from internally SUBORDINATE constructions and HEAD from MODIFYING elements within the latter. Internally coordinate constructions consisting of noun noun or verb verb will need to be charted twice (at the place where each noun or verb is entered on the chart). Internally subordinate constructions, however, will need to be charted under the head constituent (which will prove to be one of the two slots in exclusion to the other). Finally, one noun or one verb occurring as a minimal phrase will be charted in the slot recognizable as head.

Distinction of coordinate constructions versus subordinate constructions is not difficult if the two constituents of the former are joined by a coordinating conjunction (e.g., *John and Mary*). Coordinate constructions not so marked will emerge sooner or later as constructions in which (a) it is equally implausible to assume A subordinate to B or B subordinate to A, and (b) neither of the manifesting classes of the partners of the construction is more restricted than the other. The crucial question becomes, then, one of distinguishing a modifier or qualifier of some sort from a head or main element of the same broad word class. Here one follows the general principle of interpreting the more obscure data in the light of the less obscure. Thus, in any noun noun phrase construction in Trique it is highly probable that the first noun is a head while the second is a modifying element. To begin with, a parallel construction, noun plus adjective, clearly fits this pattern. Furthermore, noun noun possession phrases prepose the possessed item to the possessor, which can also be regarded as a sort of modifier. Considerations of this sort make it plausible that such a Trique phrase as $ga^3ga^3\textasciitilde$ $n\cdot e\textasciitilde e^3$ 'wire' ($ga^3ga\textasciitilde^3$ 'metal' and $n\cdot e\textasciitilde e^3$ 'rope') should be considered to mean 'rope-like metal' (with 'metal' as head) rather then 'metal rope' (with 'rope' as head).

A further question relevant to the above problem is: does the selection of tagmemes in the environment of the AB sequence prove to be conditioned by either A or by B in such a manner that one may be considered to be the ruling member rather than the other? Thus, verb-verb sequences occur in Trique. At first it was assumed that since verb-adjective sequences with main-modifier constructional meaning occurred, therefore verb-verb might also be interpreted as a main-modifier sequence in which the second verb modifies the first – thus resulting in one overall constructional pattern (head-modifier) for Trique noun and verb phrases. But the fact emerged that in a Trique verb-verb construction it is the second verb and not the first that determines selection of certain clause level tagmemes. Thus, if the second verb is transitive the whole verb phrase is transitive and may occur with an object but if the second verb is intransitive the whole verb phrase is intransitive and may not occur with an object. Furthermore, while selection of the second verb is unlimited, selection of the first verb is limited to some six/ seven verbs. Therefore in the sequence $gq^3\mathcal{P}q^{34}h$ $ga^3n\check{\imath}^{23}$ 'went' (and) erected (something)' it is the verb $ga^3n\check{\imath}^{23}$ that proves to be head with the result that the verb-verb phrase is filed and charted accordingly. Similarly, a minimal verb phrase like $ga^3n\check{\imath}^{23}$ 'erected' is charted in the column 2nd verb slot which can now be retitled main.

(2) The second problem is that of recognizing a phrase type imbedded within a phrase type. Failure to recognize such a situation leads to hopeless obscuring of the structure.

To begin with, it seems both necessary and reasonable to assume that a person who is acquainted in a practical way with the language he is analyzing, (i.e. the speaker-analyst, the language learner or one who has worked extensively with text materials) will be able to recognize a simple phrase versus a phrase suspect of containing an imbedded phrase type. Specifically, the data to which a person responds in this intuitive manner are: (a) The apparent occurrence in phrase medial of morphemes that manifest tagmas presumably phrase-initial or phrase-final. Thus in the Trique phrase $\check{z}i^3na^{45}$ ne^3h gwi^{35} zq^3-mi^3ge^2 'the cornfields-of the people of San Miguel', $\check{z}i^3na^{45}$ 'cornfield-of' is a possessed item in a phrase the rest of which indicates the possessor. A person with any practical knowledge of Trique is likely to respond to ne^3h gwi^{35} zq^3-mi^3ge^2 'the people of

San Miguel' as in some sense a whole. Notice, however, that occurrence of ne^3h 'the' in the imbedded phrase – with ne^3h 'the' regularly occurring initial in phrases nonsuspect of containing an imbedded phrase – is precisely one of the formal clues on which such intuitive response is based. (b) Occurrence more than once in a given phrase of a tagma which presumably occurs no more than once in a simple phrase. Thus in the Trique phrase $\check{c}u^3 \ ga^3ga^3? \ n\cdot e?e^3$ 'telephone pole', $\check{c}u^3$ 'wood, pole' appears to be a head element in reference to the rest of the phrase. But $ga^3ga^3?a^3$ 'metal' appears also to be head in reference to the word $n\cdot e?e^3$ 'rope, rope-like' which follows. A person acquainted with Trique could scarcely fail to make the above observation in that both $\check{c}u^3$ 'wood', and $ga^3ga^3?a^3$ 'metal' are used in many phrases as general nouns delimited and made more specific by following nouns. (c) Occurrence within the same phrase of tagmas presumably characteristic of different types of simple phrases. The following Trique phrase ilustrates this: $du^3kwa^2 \ du^{23} \ na^5ka^{53}$ '(the) house-of (the) new mayordomo'. In this phrase du^3kwa^2 'house-of' seems to manifest possessor tagma in reference to the following words. However, du^{23} 'mayordomo' seems to be a head tagma modified by na^5ka^{53} 'new'. But item-possessor and head-attribute constructions may early in one's experience with Trique be suspected of belonging to different types of phrases (e.g., possessed stems are formally distinct from unpossessed stems). It is probable that the intuitive judgment that the item-possessor phrase here includes a head-attribute phrase is based on the above distributional considerations.

If it be granted that in most cases simple phrases may be distinguished from complex phrases (i.e., from phrases including imbedded phrases), one may choose (a) to chart at first only the simple phrases (with postponement of complex phrases until simple phrases are better understood); or (b) to chart immediately both sorts of phrases. If the second alternative is followed, complex phrases should be charted as wholes, but phrases imbedded within them should be separately charted as well. Thus, in the phrase *a friend of my first cousin Gertrude*, not only should this phrase be charted as a whole (as an example of a possessive phrase) but the imbedded appositional phrase *my first cousin Gertrude* should also be charted along with its imbedded phrase *my first cousin* (as a further example of a possessive phrase). While the first alternative above seems simpler it leaves a large mass of residual data to be considered at a later stage in the analysis. Furthermore, phrase structure in many languages involves considerable imbedding of phrase type within phrase type. So marked is this multiple nesting of type within type that phrase types are sometimes partially distinguished from each other by virtue of what phrase types may occur imbedded within them. If contrastive features of this sort are to be detected, charting of complex phrases is essential to a complete analysis.

6. ANALYTICAL PROCEDURES FOR PHRASE LEVEL SYNTAGMEMES, I.E. FOR PHRASE TYPES

Here, as in section 2 for clause level syntagmemes, it is assumed that analysis of phrase level tagmemes is in process but not necessarily complete. Structural differences between phrase types are parallel to structural differences between clause types. Inasmuch as the criteria for structural differences are stated in general form in the introduction and specifically for clause in section 2, they are not repeated here.

6.1. Identify the nuclear (versus peripheral) tagmemes for each variety of phrase charted.

(1) All obligatory tagmemes are nuclear (although not all nuclear tagmemes are obligatory). Thus, in any sort of head-attribute phrase, head is obligatory and hence clearly nuclear. In an item-possessor phrase, both item and possessor are usually obligatory and hence nuclear.

(2) Tagmemes in explicit cross reference to some element in the obligatory minimum of a phrase are nuclear. Thus, in many Mayan languages, relator-axis phrases such as the equivalent of 'with John' are expressed by 'his-withness John'. The obligatory minimum of such a phrase is 'his-withness'. Epexegetical elements such as 'John' are in cross reference to the pronoun obligatory to the phrase structure. 'John' therefore manifests a further nuclear tag-

meme. In Trique verb phrases, auxiliary tagmeme, manifested by some six/seven verbs, is optional but the choice of aspect-mood in the auxiliary is so closely correlated with that of aspect-mood in the main verb that one complex aspect-mood system needs to be posited. Thus, a verb such as Pya^3h 'doing' is CONTINUATIVE as is also the auxiliary-main sequence $Pna^{35}P$ Pya^3h 'coming doing'. Likewise gi^3Pya^3h 'did' is PUNCTILIAR as is also $ga^3Pna^{35}P$ gi^3Pya^3h 'came did'. The simple verb gi^4Pya^3h 'will do' is ANTICIPATORY as is the sequence ga^5Pna^5P gi^4Pya^3h 'will come will do'. Two further aspect-moods characterize only auxiliary-main sequences: CONTINUATIVE INTENTIVE: $Pna^{35}P$ gi^4Pya^3h 'coming will do'; and PUNCTILIAR INTENTIVE: $ga^3Pna^{35}P$ gi^4Pya^3h 'came will do'. Given this involvement of aspect-mood of both auxiliary and main, it seems feasible to consider auxiliary a nuclear tagmeme.

(3) Optional tagmemes manifested by open classes tend to be nuclear while optional tagmemes manifested by small closed classes tend to be peripheral. Thus in Trique verb phrases the tagmemes adverbial (manifested by a class of five particles) and repetition (manifested only by yu^2 'again') are peripheral, while in noun phrases, identifier (manifested only by ne^3h 'identified plural') and deictic (manifested by three deictic particles) are likewise peripheral. Quantifier tagmeme in the noun phrase is manifested by numeral or numeral phrase. In the latter case we have the possibility of indefinite expansion phrase-wise into higher numerals composed of a restricted lexical inventory. It proves convenient to consider quantifier tagmeme as peripheral rather than nuclear in that this tagmeme – in spite of its phrasal expansion – still involves only a closed class of words.

(4) Nuclear tagmemes are often diagnostic of particular phrase types while peripheral tagmemes tend to occur indifferently in various phrase types.

(5) Nuclear tagmemes may be affected by transformations between phrase types or between a phrase type and some other structure; peripheral tagmemes are not. Thus, in Trique an incorporated object verb phrase is a transform of a clause structure in which the incorporated object tagmeme was once a clause level object tag-

meme, so that 'make medicine' derives from a clause in which
'medicine' was object. Incorporated object tagmeme is therefore
nuclear to its phrase type by this criterion as well as by its obligatory status.

(6) As observed for clause structure, nucleus versus periphery is
emic within a given language. Therefore initial judgment based on
criteria of the sort here given are subject to subsequent review in the
light of over-all relevance.

6.2. Separate as different phrase types any two varieties
which have at least a difference of two in the number of
nuclear tagmemes.

Thus, Bengali has several contrasting types of coordinate noun
phrases. Two such types appear quite similar in that both can generate series with indefinite number of members. Formulae follow
(all tagmemes nuclear):

$$\text{Coordinate I: } +H_1 (\pm H_2)^n +C +H_3$$
$$\text{Coordinate II: } +C_1 +H_1 +C_2 +H_2 \pm(+C_3 +H_3)^n$$

In these formulae H_1, H_2, H_3 symbolize head tagmemes manifested
by nouns, while C, C_1, C_2, and C_3 symbolize tagmemes manifested
by conjunctions. Superscript ^{n} marks a tagmeme or complex of
tagmemes as capable of indefinite repetition. C is manifested by *ar*
'and', *o* 'and', *ebɔŋ* 'and', *ba* 'or', *ɔtʿɔba* 'or', and *kimba* 'or'. C_1 is
manifested by *hoę* 'either', while C_2 and C_3 are manifsted by *nahoę*
'or'. Coordinate I is exemplified in such a construction as: *šamim,
farhat, nafis, rouzi ebɔŋ rubi* 'Shameem, Farhat, Nafees, Rosy, and
Ruby'. Coordinate II is exemplified in such a construction as:
hoę šamin nahoę farhat nahoę nafis nahoę rouzi nahoę rubi 'either
Shameem, or Farhat, or Nafees, or Rosy, or Ruby'.

A glance at the formulae indicates that these two coordinate
phrase types cannot possibly be united into one type, in that coordinate I has four nuclear tagmemes while coordinate II has six. Nor
is there sleight of hand involved in the formulization. In coordinate
I, H_2 should be considered to be nuclear if the parallel H_1 and H_3
are nuclear – as indeed they must be since they are obligatory.
Furthermore, $(\pm H_2)^n$ cannot be combined with $+H_1$ as $(H_1)^n$ in

that H_1 is obligatory while $(H_2)^n$ is optional. By a similar argument six tagmemes are seen to be nuclear in coordinate II.

6.3. Separate as different phrase types any two varieties of phrase which have a difference of one in the number of nuclear tagmemes, provided that a further structural difference is present.

The Trique repetitive verb phrase (which has two nuclear tagmemes: +main +repeated main) is by this criterion distinct from all other verb phrases in Trique. The metaphorical verb phrase has three nuclear tagmemes: ± restricted auxiliary + intransitive action + metaphorical as exemplified in na^3hwe^3 $ga^3\mathit{P}mq^3$ ru^3wa^{23} 'can't get warm inside' (i.e. 'can't get angry') and na^3ra^2h ru^3wa^{23} 'mend inside' (i.e. 'rest'). Qualifier-main also has three nuclear tagmemes: ± auxiliary + main ± modifier as in $gq^3\mathit{P}q^{34}h$ $gi^3\mathit{P}ya^3h$ $za^5\mathit{P}$ 'went did good', nga^3h $a^3to^{34}h$ $\check{z}i^5q^5\mathit{P}$ 'lying sleeping peacefully'. The incorporated object phrase likewise has three nuclear tagmemes: ± auxiliary + transitive action + incorporated object as in $\mathit{P}na^{35}\mathit{P}$ $\mathit{P}ya^3h$ $go^3no^3\mathit{P}o^2$ 'coming making medicine' and $gq^3\mathit{P}q^{34}h$ $ga^5\check{c}i^5h$ $nq^3\mathit{P}q^{34}h$ 'came will-ask word' (i.e. 'came to inquire'). For the remaining two types of Trique verb phrase, each of which also contains three nuclear tagmemes, see 6.7.

The repetitive verb phrase, in contrast to all other verb phrase types, not only has but two nuclear tagmemes but also contains a repeated main tagmeme not found elsewhere: $a^3\check{c}e^{21}$ $a^3\check{c}e^{21}$ 'walking'. Furthermore, no peripheral tagmemes occur in this phrase type.

A Chatino example illustrates peripheral elements which constitute a second structural difference. The Chatino simple predicate phrase has one nuclear tagmeme: $+\text{PrH}_1$ (predicate head$_1$) while the Chatino qualified predicate phrase has two nuclear tagmemes: $+\text{PrH}_2$ (predicate head$_2$) $+$Qn (qualification). Thus the Chatino verb $ngu\mathit{P}ni^1$ 'did' is a minimal and nuclear simple predicate phrase while $n\check{s}\psi^{43}$ $ta\mathit{P}a^{23}$ 'quarreling brother' ('fighting one another') is a minimal and nuclear qualified predicate phrase. Only certain verbs manifest Pr H_2 while many verbs manifest Pr H_1 – but this may be a collocational and lexical difference not involving classes of general relevance to Chatino grammar. Our two putative phrase types are separated, then, by but one clear structural difference. A second difference is seen in that while the simple predicate phrase (like most Chatino predicate phrases) has both a preposed and postposed periphery, the qualified predicate phrase does not have a postposed periphery except for the omnipresent ti^3 'only, just' manifesting a limitation tagmeme which closes many types of phrases. Thus, such a Chatino Pr H_1 as $ngu\mathrm{?}ni^1$ 'did' may be followed by degree tagmeme (manifested by three morphemes of which la^2 'more' is typical) and by modification tagmeme (manifested by descriptive particle or two rudimentary phrase types of very restricted structure). It is not begging the question to say that the peripheral modification tagmeme is distinct from the nuclear qualification tagmeme obligatory to its phrase type. Modification tagmeme is manifested by descriptive particles, and qualification by nouns and referential verbs. All three classes – descriptive particle, noun, and referential verb – are of general relevance to Chatino structure and hence are citable here or elsewhere as structural differences.

6.4. Separate as different phrase types any two varieties of phrase types which have the same number of nuclear tagmemes, provided that at least two nuclear tagmemes in one type contrast with two nuclear tagmemes in the other type.

The Trique qualifier-main and incorporated object verb phrases are distinct from each other by this criterion. Their nuclear tagmemes, as already stated, (6.3.), are:

Qualifier-main: ±auxiliary +main ±modifier

Incorporated object: ±auxiliary +transitive action +incorporated object

Main tagmeme, unrestricted as to transitive versus intransitive verbs, contrasts with transitive action tagmeme manifested only by transitive verbs.

Modifier tagmeme which is manifested by adjectives contrasts with incorporated object which is manifested by nouns by virtue of the (emic class) distinction between adjectives and nouns. Furthermore, incorporated object phrase is a transformation of the transitive clause while the other phrase type is not.

Bengali adjunct-head phrases and appositional phrases are distinct by this criterion. The two phrase types have the following nuclear formulae:

Adjunct-head: +adjunct +head₂

Appositional: +personal head +appositive

While all these tagmemes are manifested by nouns, the adjunct and head tagmemes are manifested only by nouns, while personal head and appositive may also be manifested by noun phrases of specifiable types. Thus, both nuclear tagmemes of each type contrast with the nuclear tagmemes of the other type. As Mohiyud-Din points out, addition of any further element to an adjunct-head phrase does not result in an expansion of this phrase type but rather transforms the phrase type to another phrase type in which adjunct-head becomes imbedded. Thus *pɔtʻ prodɔršɔk* 'road one-who-shows' is an adjunct-head phrase meaning 'guide'. Addition of a word manifesting qualifier tagmeme, such as *uttɔm* 'excellent' makes the phrase a qualifier-head phrase in which head is manifested by an imbedded adjunct-head phrase: *uttɔm pɔtʻ prodɔršɔk* 'excellent guide'. Examples of the adjunct-head phrase: *šišu šahitto* 'child literature' ('children's literature'); *rog biǰanu* 'disease germs'. Examples of appositional phrase: *kobi ǰosimuddin* 'the poet, Josimuddin'; *amra cʻatrora* 'we, the students'. In the phrase *amar bondʻu salek* 'my friend, Salek', personal head tagmeme is manifested by an imbedded possession phrase *amar bondʻu* 'my friend'.

While our two phrases are thus demonstrably distinct it is of interest to note that a further difference is seen in the fact that an appositional phrase (unique among Bengali noun phrases) is transformable to an equation clause. Thus *amar bondʻu salek* is transformable to *amar bondʻu hɔn salek* 'my friend is Salek'. It is very likely that granted presence of both an equation clause type and an appositional phrase type within a given language this transformation will be possible between the two structures.

6.5. Separate as different phrase types any two varieties of phrase which have the same number of nuclear tagmemes provided that (a) one nuclear tagmeme of the one constrasts with a nuclear tagmeme of the other and (b) a second difference can be found.

The Trique item-possessor and relator-axis phrases may be distinguished by the criterion. To one beginning the analysis of Trique, occasional homophonous manifestation of these two phrase types may obscure the difference between them. Thus, ri^3ki^3 tro^2 can mean either 'the stomach of the cow' or 'under the cow'. In both phrase types there are two nuclear tagmemes: +item +possessor and +relator +axis. In spite of the fact that eight possessed nouns (exemplified by ri^3ki^3 'stomach') may pattern in prepositional function as manifestations of relator, there is a clear difference between item and relator tagmemes. Item is manifested by obligatorily or optionally possessed nouns; relator by eight obligatorily possessed nouns, by five relational particles, and by a rudimentary phrase type involving both a relational particle and one of these eight nouns. But obligatorily and optionally possessed nouns – along with non-possessed nouns – are relevant classes in distinguishing other noun phrases from each other. Hence it is possible to count this distinction as structural here in reference to the manifestation of item tagmeme. Furthermore, the restricted manifestation of relator tagmeme sets up a closed function set which is clearly distinctive. But possessor and axis tagmeme do not contrast as to manifesting set in that either may be manifested by any noun phrase, by person enclitics, or by a relative sentence. Our second difference is found, rather, in the fact that a relator-axis phrase has no preposed periphery while a possessor phrase does. Thus, while ru^3wa^{23} da^3we^{53} means 'inside the lake' (and is relator-axis), ngo^4 ru^3wa^{23} da^3we^{53} means 'an inside of a lake'.

A second Trique example involves use of transform potential as a second structural difference. The item-possessor phrase, exemplified above, contrasts with another phrase type, person included-possessor. This contrast may be exemplified as follows: ne^3h $da^3\mathfrak{P}ni^{21}$ ngo^4 zi^{21} da^3h 'the children of a certain man' and ne^3h da^5-$\mathfrak{P}ni^5h$ ngo^4 zi^{21} da^3h 'the children of a certain man and the man himself.' In the item-possessor phrase item is manifested by $da^3\mathfrak{P}ni^{21}$ 'children-of' and in the person included-possessor phrase, person is manifested by $da^5 \bar{P}ni^5h$ 'children of (including possessor)'. There is special morphological tagging (by tone replacive morpheme) of the person tagmeme whose manifestation is restricted to certain kinship nouns. Aside from this, there is no further overt structural difference. The second structural difference resides rather in the transform potential found only in the second phrase type: person included-possessor may be transformed to a coordinate phrase as here exemplified: $ne^3h\ da^5\bar{P}ni^5h\ ngo^4\ zi^{21}\ dq^3h \rightarrow ne^3h\ da^3\bar{P}ni^{21}\ ngo^4\ zi^{21}$ $dq^3h\ nga^4\ mq^3\bar{P}q^3\ zi^3h.$ (nga^4 'with', $mq^3\bar{P}q^3$ 'oneself'. zi^3h 'he'). In this transformation, the person included-possessor phrase becomes a coordinate noun phrase the first member of which is the corresponding item-possessor phrase involving the same morphemes minus the tone replacive occurring in $da^5\bar{P}ni^5h$.

6.6. Join any two varieties of phrase not separated by a dual structural contrast (or distinguished only by lexical co-occurrence restrictions) into one phrase type with etic variants – unless strong analytical pressure require a separation.

Chatino noun phrases illustrate at one point a very marked structural difference which, nevertheless, is syntagmemically noncontrastive. The Chatino attributive phrase has the following structure: ±Qua ±Num ±dei (+H) ±att ±ch±Sta±Col±Adj ±Dem ±li (Qua = quantity, Num = number, dei = deictic, att = attribution, Ch = character, Sta = status, Col = coloration, Adj = adjectival, Dem = demonstration, li = limitation). Pride considers only head to be nuclear. Of all the tagmemes found in this phrase type only the limitation tagmeme occurs in any other phrase type. It would appear, therefore, that either this phrase type has ten nuclear tagmemes (which seems unlikely in that no other phrase type has more than three nuclear tagmemes) or else Pride is quite correct in making only the head tagmeme nuclear. There is, however, a variety of this phrase in which rather than any of the seven postposed peripheral tagmemes given above there occurs an imbedded descriptive clause or sentence. Thus, there is marked difference in postposed peripheries: either a string of seven tagmemes or another mutually exclusive tagmeme which Pride calls descriptive. In spite of this structural difference Pride considers these two varieties of phrase to be subtypes. Her decision can be defended on the ground that (a) the contrast is entirely peripheral and effects nowhere the nucleus of the phrase type; while (b) the mutually exclusive distribution of descriptive tagmeme with the other seven postposed tagmemes seems clearly to be a mechanical result of the length and complexity of the manifestation of the descriptive tagmeme, i.e. granted presence of the imbedded clause or sentence manifesting descriptive, there is scarcely room for any other postposed phrase level tagmeme.

Presumably, sufficient analogical pressure could result in two varieties of phrases being separated into two phrase types even in the absence of an adequate dual structural contrast. For such a situation on the clause level, see 2.7. above. Such analogies could best be seen in a matrix such as suggested in the following procedure.

6.7. Arrange partially similar but systematically contrasting phrase types in one or more matrices with appropriate dimensions.

Thus five Trique verb phrases may be arranged in the following matrix – while a sixth type of verb phrase remains extra-systemic:

	Unaugmented Nucleus:	Augmented Nucleus:	Nucleus $\subset$ ru^3wa^{23}:
Unrestricted Auxiliary:	Active Qualifier-Main	Incorporated Object	
Restricted Auxiliary:	Nonactive Qualifier-Main	Incorporated Complement	Metaphorical

Phrases with unrestricted auxiliary take two sets of auxiliaries, i.e. motion (e.g., 'come', 'go', 'walk'), and abilitative auxiliaries ('can', 'can't'). Phrases with restricted auxiliary take only abilitative auxiliaries and those only on the condition that the main verb be punctiliar in aspect. Unaugmented nuclei contain besides the auxiliary only main and modifier tagmemes. Augmented nuclei do not contain modifier tagmeme but contain rather a phrase level tagmeme that is a transform of some clause level tagmeme which has fallen into the nucleus of the clause. Active qualifier-main phrases have been illustrated in 6.3. Nonactive qualifier-main phrases contain either a copula or a meteorological verb as main and contain three subtypes: (1) True copulative phrases; which may have only $\check{z}a^5nga^5\mathcal{P}$ 'truly' and ge^5 'sure enough' as modifier: $w\cdot\underline{\imath}^3$ $\check{z}a^5nga^5\mathcal{P}$ 'truly be' $na^3\mathcal{P}we^3$ $ga^4w\underline{\imath}^3$ 'can't become', $ga^3\mathcal{P}we^3$ $ga^4w\underline{\imath}^3$ $\check{z}a^5nga^5\mathcal{P}$ 'truly can become'. (2) Pseudo-copulative (descriptive phrases) take a wide variety of adjectives as modifier: $w\cdot\underline{\imath}^3$ $za^5\mathcal{P}$ 'be good', $na^3\mathcal{P}we^3$ $gq^3w\underline{\imath}^3$ ga^5ci^5 'can't be white'. (3) Meteorological phrases have limited lexical selections of modifier: $ga^3mq^{35}\mathcal{P}$ ni^4ko^3 'rained plentifully', $na^3\mathcal{P}we^3$ $ga^5mq^5\mathcal{P}$ 'can't rain'.

Incorporated object phrases have also been illustrated in 6.3. Incorporated complement verb phrase is a rare type: $ga^4w\underline{\imath}^3$ $dre^3h\text{-}e^3h$ $re^5\mathcal{P}$ (yu^5h) 'will-become father-pl. you' (I), i.e., '(I'll) become your father', and $ga^3w\underline{\imath}^3$ ni^3ka^4 $re^5\mathcal{P}$ $(mq^3\mathcal{P}q^3)$ 'became wife yours (she)' i.e. '(she) became your wife'. Incorporated complement is manifested by an imbedded possession phrase and is a transform of clause level complement tagmeme of the equative clause. Metaphorical phrase has also been illustrated in 6.3.

Extra-systemic to the above matrix is a sixth Trique verb phrase type, the repetitive phrase. This phrase type contains but two nuclear tagmemes (+main +repeated main) without periphery: $a^3\check{c}e^{21}$ $a^3\check{c}e^{21}$ 'walking, walking', $ni^3\mathcal{P}ya^{34}h$ $ni^3\mathcal{P}ya^{34}h$ 'looking, looking'. The verb, if marked for aspect, is continuative and the meaning of the phrase type is emphatic continuative.

6.8. Inspect the posited matrix or matrices for (a) confirmation of types already posited, and (b) clues as to possible further types.

Thus, inspecting the matrix for Trique verb phrases above we might seek for a possible phrase type with unrestricted auxiliary yet containing either ru^3wa^{23} (metaphorical modifier) or some similar element. The sequence rq^2h ru^3wa^{23} 'accuse' might be suspect of manifesting such a further phrase type in that it apparently contains ru^3wa^{23} which may take a motion auxiliary: $gq^3\mathcal{P}q^{34}h$ gi^3rq^2h ru^3wa^{23} 'went accused'. But, in that this phrase has nothing to parallel it we might better consider it to be an active qualifier-main phrase with a ru^3wa^{23} element of uncertain meaning homophonous with ru^3wa^{23} 'metaphorical modifier'.

7. ANALYTICAL PROCEDURES FOR PHRASE LEVEL TAGMEMES

7.0.1. Prepare an exhaustive list of the items or sequences comprising the set manifesting each phrase level tagma whenever that set is not readily summarizable.

7.0.2. Attempt to summarize in statement form the items and sequences manifesting each tagma. Thus the items manifesting main tagma of the Trique active qualifier-main verb phrase might be summarized: "Presumably all verbs except copulative, meteorological, and emphatic verbs."[1] The filler of auxiliary tagmeme of the same verb phrase type could be summarized as "certain intransitive verbs in two subclasses: motion, and abilitative". The fillers of head, item, and person tagmas in various Trique noun phrase types could be distinguished in similar fashion: occurrence of unpossessed and optionally possessed nouns in head; occurrences of optionally possessed and obligatorily possessed nouns in item; occurrence of particular obligatorily possessed nouns (kinship terms) in person.

It is important to note which phrase level tagmemes may be manifested by imbedded phrases and to list possible phrase types so occurring. In many languages the phrase level is characterized by multiple nesting of phrase type within phrase type. Thus, in many languages a possession phrase may occur within a possession phrase up to an unspecified number of layers limited only by the discretion of the speaker: cf. English *John's mother's sister's son* and Ogden Nash's *friend of a friend of a friend of a friend*.

7.0.3. In performing these listing and summarizing procedures the analyst may discover inconsistencies in regard to his tentative identification of phrase level

---

[1] Emphatic verbs are a class of verbs relevant here and on the sentence level where they figure in emphasis-affirmation colons; cf. 15.1.(3).

tagmas or in regard to the charting of them. Here, as in
3.0.3., appropriate rectification should be made.

7.1. List as tagmemically separate the tagmas that without further analysis already appear to be unequivocably
distinct from each other on distributional-semantic
grounds. Thus, the nuclear tagmemes of any phrase type are
distinguishable from each other and from all peripheral tagmemes
of the same string on such grounds as (compare 3.1.): (a) distinctive
physical positions, (b) difference in obligatory versus optional status; (c) distinctive manifestations in terms of word classes, (d)
distinctive manifestations in terms of word types, imbedded phrase
types, or subordinate clauses, (e) distinctive cross reference to a core
tagmeme or agreement with such a tagmeme; (f) distinctive transforms.

7.2. Look within the same phrase type for pairs of tagmas that are suspect of being the same tagmeme in that
they exhibit similarities in respect to one or more of the
following considerations: manifesting set, internal structure
(whether word or imbedded phrase), slot meaning, and position(s)
of occurrence. Rather than attempting to set up here a list of suspect phrase level tagmas, we content ourselves with the observation
that here, as in clause structure, any two tagmas should be considered mutually suspect if they are causing analytical difficulties.
For example, in the charting procedure advocated above the analyst
may find himself inconsistently and arbitrarily assigning the same
or very similar elements to first one tagma and then to another within the same string. In the analysis of the Jacaltec noun phrase
Clarence and Kay Church had considerable difficulty distinguishing
CLASSIFIER tagma from HEAD tagma (with a correlating confusion of
head and modifier tagmas). That some sort of classifier tagma was
present in the Jacaltec noun phrase seemed probable in that a dozen
or so morphemes seemed to be used in such a classifier function.
Thus, *čʔen* 'referring to objects of stone, metal, and metal-like
materials' is used in such phrases as the following: *čʔen vasu* 'the
(mineral-class) water glass'; *čʔen ši* 'the (mineral-class) teakettle';
čʔen avion 'the (mineral-class) airplane'; and even *čʔen čʔen* 'the

(mineral-class) rock'. But difficulty was occasioned by the fact that the sets manifesting classifier and head tagmas apparently overlapped to some degree (compare the last example above). Therefore, while *nah* seemed to serve as a classifier for masculine in some phrases, e.g. in *nah ča* 'the (male-class) smallpox', yet in other phrases it certainly served as head, e.g., *heb nah* 'the men' (*heb* 'plural specifier', *nah* 'man'). There were, therefore, phrases which could be analyzed as containing either a classifier-head tagma sequence or a head-modifier sequence (e.g., *hun nah luhwum* 'one (male) fisherman'; *hun* 'one' *nah* 'male/man', *luhwum* 'fisherman'). For this reason classifier and head needed to be treated as a pair of suspect tagmas in Jacaltec along with a second such suspect pair consisting of head and modifier. For a while the possibility was entertained of eliminating the classifier tagma altogether.

7.3. Join as one tagmeme any two tagmas suspect of being the same tagmeme provided that they occur in noncontrastive distribution in the same phrase type. Thus one adverbial tagmeme manifested by five particles has been set up in all five types of Trique verb phrase. For some time, however, it seemed that two of these particles nu^3 'negative' and zi^4 'cohortative negative' might manifest a separate negative tagmeme. But further study has indicated that the tagma manifested by these two negative particles should be combined with the tagma manifested by the other three; $a^5ʔ$ 'already', u^3ta^4 'very, much', ru^3wa^{23} 'almost, about to'. One and only one of any five of these particles may occur; the negative particles are mutually exclusive not only with each other but with the other three particles as well. Furthermore, three of the five particles have a common characteristic of affecting the selection of the tense and aspect of the verb which manifests main. Thus $a^5ʔ$ 'already' selects a verb in indicative mood; ru^3wa^{23} 'almost' selects a verb in punctiliar aspect, anticipatory mood; and zi^4 'let not, will not', selects punctiliar aspect, indicative mood regardless of the tense implications of the situation.

7.4. Separate tagmemically any two suspect tagmas that occur in the same phrase type, but which may both occur in a given phrase provided that there is also some semantically significant difference in the mutual ordering of the two tagmas or in manifesting set.

Thus the pair of Jacaltec suspect tagmas (classifier vs. head) described above in 7.2. are separated as follows: (a) There is a class of fifteen classifier nouns each of which is distinguished from other nouns by at least two of the following three criteria: (1) They may occur in repeat sequence as *čʔen čʔen* 'the rock'. (2) They are never possessed. (3) They fill a pronominal function in paragraph structure so that while 'horse' may be introduced into the first part of a paragraph as *noʔ če* 'animal-class horse', the classifier *noʔ* alone will be used in the balance of the paragraph unless the whole phrase be used again for clarity or emphasis. (b) Classifier occurs before head and any item following head is modifier. A sequence analytically ambiguous as to head-modifier-modifier analysis versus classifier-head-modifier analysis is considered to be the latter in that aside from such ambiguous sequences there seem to be no occurrences of more than one modifier in a given phrase. In that the classifier-head construction is found to be extremely common in Jacaltec, sequences analytically ambiguous as to classifier-head versus head-modifier are considered to be the former. Nevertheless, such data as these emphasize that an area of analytic indeterminacy may exist side by side with a demonstrable structural distinction.

7.5. Consider that a repeat sequence of the same tagmeme is constituted by two (or more) suspect tagmas that occur in continuous or discontinuous sequence in the same phrase without a semantically significant difference in order or in manifesting set.

In English, there are several tagmemes that precede the head in the modifier-head phrase: identifier manifested by articles *a* and *the* and possibly a few other items; quantity manifested by numerals and numeral-like words; size (including duration) manifested by such words as *great, huge, sudden, quick, narrow, long,* and others; condition manifested by adjectives and participles; color manifested by color adjectives; style-material by such words as *portable, steel, silk*; and name manifested by items in close immediate constituent tie grammatically and lexically with a following head (e.g. *scrap iron, merchant marine*, *Ford car*, *storage batteries*, *hoisting boom*. Thus we have such phrases as: *a soft green jersey dress* (identifier, condition, color, name, head), *a quick secret flash* (identifier, size, condition, head), *the three little black notebrooks* (identifier, quantity, size, color, head), and *attractive, orange-colored, glass mantel pieces* (condition, color, material, name, head). Order is not rigid everywhere in the above; e.g. while *eager black waters* follows the usual order, *black eager waters* gains intensity by inverting the order. Similarly, the word *little* manifesting size is likely to follow condition as in *a sorry little procession*. Some of these tagmemes may occur more than once. Thus in the following examples, condition occurs twice: *unresisting, ship-wrecked Japanese* and *a decent, untarnished man*. Similarly size may occur more than once: *the narrow, low, filth-choked entrance* (identifier, size, size, condition, head).

7.6. Look for sequences of tagmas that are suspect of being not two distinct phrase level tagmemes but only one phrase level tagmeme manifested by a lower level syntagmeme, i.e. a word or stem structure.

Trique sequences as gwi^{53} $\check{z}a^5na^{53}$ 'woman', zi^3 $\check{z}a^5na^{53}$ 'young woman' and zi^3 $na^4\mathcal{P}u^{43}$ 'man' (gwi^{35} 'person, zi^3 'young person, man', $\check{z}a^5na^{53}$ 'female', $na^4\mathcal{P}u^{43}$ 'male') would at first glance appear to be phrases of head-attribute structure. Nevertheless, they are peculiar in that they may be followed by another attribute: gwi^{35} $\check{z}a^5na^5$ $za\mathcal{P}a^{53}$ 'good woman', and zi^3 $na^4\mathcal{P}u^4$ ni^4ki^3 'unfortunate man'. Aside from a few such examples as these, a head is not followed by two attributives. The possibility should, therefore, be entertained that gwi^{35} $\check{z}a^5na^5$ 'woman' and the other two sequences are grammatically on a level of structure lower than the phrase, viz, word or stem structure, in spite of the fact that they display no special phonological cohesion.

The Trique sequence gwi^3 $gq^5\mathcal{P}q^3h$ 'day fourth', i.e., 'Thursday', is similarly suspect. One frequently hears gwi^3 gwi^3 $gq^5\mathcal{P}q^3h$ '(the) day Thursday' in which gwi^3 'day' occurs twice in a manner that we might not expect it to occur if the second gwi^3 were not grammatically compounded with the stem for 'fourth'. Furthermore, names for other days of the week contain phonologically deviant forms for 'day' which indicate some special phonological cohesion; e.g. $gwe^3 Pngo^{53}$ 'day first, Monday', gu^3ihi^{53} 'day second, Tuesday'.

Two other Trique sequences are similarly suspect on phonological grounds: $da^3 Pni^{45} \ \check{z}a^5na^{53}$ 'daughter' and $da^3 Pni^{45} \ zna^4 Pu^{43}$ 'son' ($< da^3 Pni^{21}$ 'child-of', $\check{z}a^5na^{54}$ 'female', $zna^4 Pu^{43}$ 'male'). Noun-adjective sequences with final ^{45} on the noun are very rare and typically involve constituents of uncertain meaning (although not in the two examples given here). Furthermore, possession phrases with an attribute intervening between item and possessor are rare.

7.7. **Join such a suspect sequence of tagmas into one phrase level tagmeme whenever overall tactical considerations make it simpler to posit further complications on a lower level (word or stem) than on the phrase level itself.**

Thus, the first two Trique problems presented above in 7.6. emerge grammatically as derivative formations which can be allocated to a level of stem formation in Trique. By adopting this analysis we need not – on the basis of highly restricted data – modify our generalization that a head tagmeme is followed by one and only one attribute in the head-qualifier noun phrase. The sequence gwi^{35} $\check{z}a^5na^5$ 'woman' is not therefore a head-attribute phrase but a stem. The day names also emerge as stem structures because of the peculiar preposing of gwi^3 'day' to phrases involving gwi^3 – often with special phonological modification of the second.

Overall tactical considerations do not, however, make it feasible to consider $da^3 Pni^{45} \ \check{z}a^5na^{54}$ 'daughter' and $da^3 Pni^{45} \ zna^4 Pu^{43}$ 'son' to be stems. Although possession phrases with an element interposed between item and possessor are rare, they nevertheless occur: $da^3 Pni^{45} \ \check{z}a^5na^5 \ zi^3$ 'his daughter', $da^3 Pni^{45} \ zna^4 Pu^{43} \ zi^3$ 'his son', $da^3 Pni^{45} \ zi^5 Pni^5 \ zi^3$ 'his granddaughter', $da^3 Pni^{45} \ zi^3 \ ga^3ta^{34}h \ zi^3$ 'his son-in-law', $da^3 Pni^{45} \ \check{z}a^5ko^5 P \ zi^3$ 'his daughter-in-law', $da^3 Pni^{45} \ ma^3ne^2 \ zi^3$ 'his god-child', and $da^3 Pni^{45} \ gq^5 Pq^5 \ zi^3$ 'his step-child'. Nor are all such items kinship terms; $zi^3u^{34} \ da^3kwe^2h$ 'vulva' (zi^3u^{34} 'bodily orifice', da^3kwe^2h 'mucus') occurs as well. Here, it seems best to set up a further type of possession phrase with + item +attribute

+possessor structure and with an item tagmeme frequently manifested by nouns bearing the peculiar fossilized [45] tone pattern.

8. CONCLUDING PROCEDURES FOR PHRASE LEVEL ANALYSIS (SUMMARY, EXPANSION, AND CROSS-CHECKING)

8.1. Residue should now be reexamined in the light of the analysis of phrase level syntagmemes and tagmemes obtained by the above procedures. Each residual tagma must be assigned to a tagmeme already analyzed or a new tagmeme must be posited. Phrases by-passed as too difficult for beginning analysis must be analyzed as: (a) phrase types already posited but with intricate internal nesting of imbedded phrases (or subordinate clauses) or (b) as new phrase types, i.e. one or more previously unanalyzed syntagmemes. See 5.6.(a) for criteria for recognizing included phrases. Subordinate clauses (manifesting perhaps some sort of attribute tagmeme) are recognizable and analyzable as per 1-4 above.

8.2. Write a brief summary sketch of phrase level syntagmemes and tagmemes of the language. For each phrase type and each phrase level tagmeme give identifying-contrastive features similar to those suggested for the clause in 4.2.

8.3. Check rapidly the above description of phrase structure against a larger corpus. Look only for data that adds to, clarifies, or modifies the description (cf. 4.3.).

8.4. Revise the description to account for the fuller corpus and write up the phrase structure in more complete and elegant form.

III

WORD LEVEL PROCEDURES

9. PRELIMINARY PROCEDURES FOR WORD LEVEL ANALYSIS

Use both elicited forms and text material to build up a corpus of words. Forms found in text are less suspect of being distorted or artificially expanded than elicited froms, but it is usually difficult to construct a word paradigm from text material in that occurrences of given stems with given affixes is fortuitous. It is profitable, therefore, to spot check elicited forms against forms found in text and to use forms found in text as clues to further forms that need to be elicited. For distribution of words in higher grammatical units text material is indispensable.

9.0. Definition of word: a class of syntagmemes of a comparatively low hierarchical order, ranking below such syntagmemes as the phrase and clause and above such syntagmemes as the stem (as well as above roots which have no internal structure and are therefore not syntagmemes). It may be of greatly varied structure (single-centered: *neglected, greenhouse*; double-centered: *foot-pound, choo-choo*; or noncentered: *overhead, undersea*) and express a multiplicity of relationships (compare *outcast, outcome, outdoor, outfield,* and *outside*). Words tend to be rigidly ordered linear sequences containing tagmemes which (aside from those manifested by stems) are manifested by closed classes of morphemes unexpandable into morpheme sequences and giving only stereotyped bits of information.

Words are typically stem-affix strings having rigidly ordered component parts. Although the stem may be complex (and may in fact be a separate grammatical level) the affixes typically are minimum recurring partials, i.e. morphs which may be grouped into morphemes. The information given by the affixes is usually information of a rather rudimentary variety in contrast to that given on the phrase and the clause levels. Thus, although a verb may include a tense tagmeme (manifested by a small, closed class of morphemes not expandable to morpheme sequences) a clause level tense tagmeme may be manifested by items and sequences of considerable complexity and variety, such as *yesterday at about* 4.00 *PM by naval observatory time, or in the remote past before the chalcolithic horizon in the Near East.*

We reject here Bloomfield's definition of word as a 'minimum free form' (*Language*, 178). Rather, we would term minimum free forms words only when such forms are capable of word-level expansion (e.g. by affixation). Otherwise, minimum free forms are simply roots (e.g. English *of, the, there, rather*). While any word structure contains one or more roots, a language will probably have some free roots not expandable into word structures. Such usage of the terms word and root reserves the former for sequences displaying internal grammatical structure on a level lower than that of the phrase. On a still lower level – but nevertheless one displaying internal structure – stem may be posited in many languages.

Nouns and verbs in many languages will prove to be classes embracing both words and (free) roots, i.e. inflected and uninflected forms, or even classes embracing words, stems, and roots. This is not in itself awkward in that the noun-verb distinction certainly is applicable to more than one structural level. The various types of phrases found in a language may be classified as noun phrases, verb phrases, and the like. Furthermore, in some languages clause types may be classified as nominal and verbal as well (cf. Hebrew). Not only may roots be classified in the grammar of a language but contrasting syntagmemes on various levels may be so classified as well. The roots which we ultimately reach in the analysis of a language are not a level as such in that they display neither internal structure nor contrasting types. Roots may not even be classifiable in some languages (e.g. Malayo-Polynesian) where they are building blocks entering indifferently into the structure of various contrasting types (so that verbs and nouns are built on the same stock of roots).

9.1. Isolate word units. In a language where both phrase and word are emic grammatical levels, word units are bounded by the borders of phrase level tagmemes. Every sequence of phonemes thus bounded is a word unless it has an internal tagmemic structure which requires us to consider it to be a syntagmeme on some other level (e.g. phrase or clause); or unless it proves to be a root. Thus, in the English phrase, *the cheerless neglected men* we indicate with vertical lines borders of phrase level tagmemes: *the* | *cheerless* | *neglected* | *men*. The last three units marked off by vertical lines are English word structures in that (1) they are bounded by borders of phrase level tagmemes; and (2) no unit thus bounded has a structure which requires our considering it to be an English phrase or clause. The first unit *the* is unexpandable and is therefore simply a root. Similarly, we indicate with vertical lines phrase level tagmemes in another English phrase: *the* | *beliefs* | *of this sect*. Here, however, while *the* and *beliefs* are immediately identifiable as root and word respectively, *of this sect* has a structure which requires us to consider it an English phrase nesting within the larger phrase. Drawing vertical lines within *of this sect* we obtain, however, *of*, *this*, and *sect* as English roots and words. In the phrase *all large species which are found east of the Rockies*, boundaries of phrase level tagmemes mark off *all*, *large*, and *species* as roots and words but leave a sequence *which are found east of the Rockies*. In that this latter sequence has the structure of an English clause, the analyst must first mark off boundaries of clause level tagmemes – thus obtaining phrases (and the non-phrase-forming word *which*, see 5.1.). It will then be possible to proceed as here indicated; when no further included phrase or clause structures are found the remaining units will be roots and words.

By this criterion, certain phonologically bound forms are considered to be roots or words. Thus, in the English sentence *Frank's the one*, the bound form -'s manifests clause level predicate tagmeme. Furthermore, as head tagmeme of a minimal verb phrase (phrases with the verb *be* as the head are expandable to such structures as *would have been* and *shall be*) -'s is bounded by borders of phrase level tagmemes. This bound form is a word in that it is an inflected form. This is rather obvious in English in that the bound form varies to a free form *is* in more precise speech. There are languages, however, where certain bound forms not readily identifiable as variants of free forms also manifest phrase level tagmemes. In Trique, the possessor tagmeme in item-possessor noun phrases may be manifested by either (a) noun phrase, or (b) pronoun phrase, or (c) tone substitution. The form $da^3 \widehat{P}ni^3$ 'son-her' i.e. 'her son' – although consisting of a stem $da^3 \widehat{P}ni^{21}$ plus ^{3} tone substitution marking third person – is grammatically parallel to $da^3 \widehat{P}ni^{21}$ zi^{21} $d\varrho^3h$ 'son-of man that'. The tone substitution marking third person occurs only in the absence of some free element or sequence marking third person. The tone substitution is equivalent, therefore, to a minimal noun or pronoun phrase. Grammatically, such tone substitutions are roots rather than words (in that they have no internal grammatical structure). Phonologically, however, they need to be considered constituents of phonological words.

In languages where the phonological stress-juncture group coincides rather closely with the grammatical word, phonological features may be helpful in delineating the boundaries of roots and grammatical words. Such phonological clues must not be followed blindly but employed with a critical awareness that even in a language with a high degree of correlation between phonological and grammatical boundaries there may still exist mutual skewness of phonology and grammar at one or more points.

9.2. Isolate recurring partials (morphs) found in the words of the corpus. Morphemic and morphophonemic considerations are relevant here only as they bear on the tagmemic structure of words: for a more adequate treatment of these subjects the reader is referred to one of the standard texts. In that the word is a comparatively low-level structure it follows that the bulk of its tagmemes will be manifested by minimum recurring partials (aside from stems which are usually characterized by open class membership and may be morphemically complex). Identification of such recurring partials is crucial to the identification of word level tagmemes. Since, however, our goal is the identification of these tagmemes, we may rightly allow this goal to influence the cutting into morphs. Thus, we do not want to posit an EMPTY morph (see

Hockett, *Language* 23.333) if there is no tagmeme which it is considered to manifest. On the other hand, when the tagmemic analysis calls for two tagmemes and but one morph occurs we will not hesitate to posit a PORTMANTEAU morph (Hockett, *Language* 23.333) manifesting the two morphemes required by the tagmemic analysis. We will not bother to analyze out all resemblant recurring partials if we find that further cutting does not seem fruitful for tagmemic analysis.[1] Grouping of morphs into morphemes is relevant to tag-

[1] Pike, in two articles to be published soon ("Theoretical Implications of Matrix Permutation in Fore (New Guinea)", *Anthropological Linguistics*; and "Conflated Field Structures in Potawatomi and Arabic", with Barbara Erickson as co-author, *International Journal of American Linguistics*) takes up in highly sophisticated fashion questions of ill-defined morphemic contrasts. He arrives at a componential analysis (of the sort rejected for Hebrew in 11.6) which largely by-passes questions of morphemic identification. Apparently a tagmemic analysis of such word structures (Fore of New Guinea, and Potawatomi of North America) would not distinguish separate tagmemes when categories (person and number in Fore, person of subject plus person of object in Potawatomi) are so fused that no analysis yields regular form-meaning components which can be considered to be manifestations of separate tagmemes. Since we are interested in setting up morphemes with a view towards grammatical analysis (rather then lexical analysis) we therefore refuse to distinguish separate morphemes under such conditions of fusion or portmanteau manifestation. Thus, Pike presents Fore object prefixes as follows (1, 2. and 3 stand for persons, S, P, and D stand for 'singular', 'plural', and 'dual');

	1	2	3
S	na-	ka-	a-
P	ta-	ti-	i-
D	tasi-	tisi-	isi-

In terms of unions and intersections of semantic categories Pike analyzes the following components:

$$a- \ = \ 1 \cup S$$
$$i- \ = \ (2 \cup 3) \cap (P \cup D)$$
$$t- \ = \ (1 \cup 2) \cap (P \cup D)$$
$$\# \ = \ 3 \cap (S \cup P \cup D)$$
$$k- \ = \ 2 \cap S$$
$$n- \ = \ 1 \cap S$$

As an analysis of lexical components the above is relevant and interesting. In terms of tagmemic structure, however, we distinguish but two tagmemes, person-number and dual. Person-number is manifested by the following morphemes: na-, ka-, a-, ta-, ti-, i-. Dual, which optionally followed the last three morphemes is manifested by si-.

The fact that two tagmemes are separate on a higher level does not imply that these two need be separate on a lower level. Thus, while Potawatomi distinguishes subject and object as clause level tagmemes, unitary prefixes mark but

memic analysis in that such grouping enables us to assert that the same set of morphemes actualizes occurrence of a given word level tagmeme in varying environments even though the form of the morphemes is not identical in all environments. Thus, in those English nouns which mark plural, we want to be able to say that such nouns have two word level tagmemes, a noun stem plus number tagmeme with both overt (plural) and covert (singular) manifestations (cf. 2.7.). It is convenient to refer to the overt manifestation of this tagmeme as one pluralizing morpheme even though English plurals are notoriously irregular.

Tagmemics, in keeping with its orientation towards Pike's tri-modal structuring of linguistic units, insists on a manifestation for every linguistic unit. It follows then, that no unit consists wholly of zero. A zero allomorph of a morpheme – provided one and only one zero occurs – is tolerated. A zero morpheme is not allowed in that this would be equivalent to setting up a unit manifested wholly by zero. Nevertheless, one zero allotagma of a tagmeme is allowed provided that the tagmeme otherwise is overtly marked. Thus, in one tense of the Hebrew verb (the imperfect or preformative tense) there is a person-number-gender category (3d person singular masculine) marked by zero. We do not set up here a zero morpheme to mark this person-number-gender category, but rather set up a zero allotagma of the person-number-gender tagmeme which is otherwise overtly marked.

9.3. Copy out on 3 × 5 slips examples of use of each stem with varied patterns of affixal combination. Only one word should be written on each slip (to facilitate future grouping); and accurate location in the corpus should be given. In a language with a relatively small amount of affixation many stems with all observed patterns of affix combination may be filed. In a language with one

---

one person-of-subject-and-object tagmeme on the word level. In the latter there is no question of "fusion "of morphs. The recurring partials are simple and of one phoneme length; only the meanings are complicated (4 stands for obviative person):

k-	=	1,3,4, subject with 2 object; or vice versa.
n-	=	3,4 subject with 1 object; or vice versa.
w-	=	4 subject with 3 object; or vice versa.

or more word types characterized by a multiplicity of affix combinations (with, say, several thousand forms possible for each verb) such exhaustive filing may not be feasible. In such circumstances care must be taken to make the file representative of the corpus lest one or more word types remain undiscovered and unanalyzed because of the analyst's preoccupation with extensive exploration of other stem-affix combinations. Nevertheless, with full consciousness of this danger the analyst may have to content himself with a rather thorough exploration of paradigms involving a relatively small number of stems along with spot-checking of other stems which seem to be similar to those more thoroughly studied.

9.4. File the slips in some fashion so as to bring together all words involving the same stem (or root or base). This may be accomplished by alphabetizing according to (a) form of stem, (b) hypothetical stem form, or (c) by English translation (with a certain inevitable inconsistency in filing in the latter case).

9.5. Inspect each group of slips for gaps in the data and elicit further forms where necessary.

9.6. Charting procedures. In that word structures typically are sequences characterized by rather rigid internal ordering, charting is especially crucial to their analysis. Various sorts of charting procedures are here suggested with a view towards their applicability to varieties of word structure. In some languages identification of relative orders of affixes gives us the word level tagmemes without further analysis. In other languages relative ordering is found to be not entirely indicative of functional distinctions and adjustments must be made as suggested in subsequent procedures.

9.6.1. Make a guess as to the number of separate charts that will handle the data well. Not only will nouns and verbs need to be charted separately but there may be different sorts of nouns and different sorts of verbs all of which need separate charting. Pike comments as follows on the article "Candoshi Verb Inflection" by Doris Cox:

"One is not justified in assuming that it is useful to make a single chart showing the relative order of the affixes of all the verbs of a language. This is tantamount to assuming that all the verbs constitute a single structure. The Cox material showed very clearly that an attempt to include all the inflectional orders of the verb on a single chart led to disadvantages in a number of ways. It made the material unwieldy, because of the large number of orders, but much more serious was the fact that it implied a great many falsehoods. By seeing all these relative orders on a single chart the reader is encouraged to assume that potentially a word could be made up of any combination of affixes from the various orders of the chart. This is sometimes – as in the Candoshi material of Cox – very far from being the empirical situation. On the contrary, the obligatory elements for different kinds of verbs may differ, and the restrictions as to which affixes may go with the obligatory components of these verb types may differ sharply, even while overlapping." ((Pike, *IJAL* 23.120-1.)

In guessing as to the number of separate charts that may be needed, the following may be helpful: (1) Impressionistic judgments already gained by elicitation, filing of data, and speaking a language may provide clues. For example, one may know that given the presence of one certain affix a verb form is relatively short but given the presence of another affix a verb form may be much more extensive. Such clues as this may be indicative of two structurally different strings that need separate charting. (2) Different sorts of nouns may have as focal such distinctions as animate versus inanimate, possessed versus unpossessed, definite versus indefinite, proper versus common, honorific versus nonhonorific. (3) Different sorts of verbs may have as focal such distinctions as : transitive versus intransitive, active versus passive, indicative versus some other mode or modes, independent versus dependent, interrogative or imperative versus declarative, negative versus affirmative. (4) Adjectives, adverbs, pronouns, numerals, demonstratives, participles, and particles may each need separate charting. (5) Last, but by no means least, external distribution of words in nuclear position in phrase types and clause types of radically different structure may provide a presumption that the words belong to different word types.

Some margin of error is inevitable in any preliminary judgments of this sort. Should two structurally distinct word types be inadvertently charted together, this will become evident in the course of the charting and lead to eventual division of the chart. Conversely, should the same word type be inadvertently charted in two or more charts the essential structural identity of the two will eventually emerge and lead to their being united.

9.6.2. For each group of words to be charted separately plot the relative orders of suffixes (if present), reckoning from the stem outward.

(1) On a ruled sheet with vertical columns and horizontal rows, label the first column "Reference", and number successively as many further columns as you guess may prove to be relevant. (2) In the first numbered column list in as many rows as necessary any morpheme(s) occurring only adjacent to the stem without any other morpheme ever intervening. For each morpheme indicate in the Reference column the location of relevant examples in your corpus. These morphemes are first order. (3) In the second numbered column, list in other successive rows farther down on the page, any morpheme(s) occurring (a) immediately following morphemes of the first order or (b) immediately following first order morphemes in some words and immediately following the stem in others. Indicate in the Reference column the location of examples in your corpus. These morphemes are second order. (4) In the third numbered column and in other rows still further down on the page list any morpheme(s) occurring (a) immediately following morphemes of the second order or (b) immediately following second order morphemes in some words and immediately following the stem and/or first order morphemes in other words. Indicate in the Reference column the location of examples. These morphemes are third order. (5) Continue in this manner, using additional columns and rows to list as many orders as are needed to account for all morphemes occurring as suffixes in the group of words being charted.

Your chart will look somewhat as follows:

Reference	1.	2.	3.	4.	5.
p. 12, l. 6	-t				
p. 1, l. 1		-opo			
p. 35, l. 4		-are			
p. 12, l. 10			-n		
p. 20, l. 9			-man		
p. 19, l. 7			-l		
p. 19. l, 8				-I	
p. 31, l. 14					-ik

9.6.3. Inspect the resultant scheme for plausibility. (1) Note which morphemes are obligatory and which are optional; note consistency or inconsistency of grouping of such morphemes in relative orders. (2) Note which morphemes may occur word final and which must occur word final. Are such morphemes grouped plausibly or scattered? Do some "final" morphemes occur early in the scheme of relative orders? (3) Note which morphemes are mutually exclusive in the same form. Are such morphemes grouped plausibly? (4) Is the occurrence of certain morphemes dependent on the occurrence of other morphemes? If so, does the scheme obtained in 9.6.2. seem consonant with this mutual dependency? (5) In brief, is each of the posited relative orders characterized by morphemes apparently homogeneous in function or by rather heterogeneous elements? (The latter may be true of certain relative orders in word structures in some languages but should always be carefully rechecked before being accepted as a linguistic fact of life.)

If any persistent difficulty is encountered the following additional procedures should be employed (especially in languages with heavy affixation):

9.6.4. Plot the relative orders of suffixes, reckoning from word final backwards towards the stem.

(1) On a sheet of paper ruled as in 9.6.2. label the last column on the right "Reference", and number off from right to left as many further columns as may prove necessary. (2) In the first numbered column list in as many rows as necessary any morpheme(s) occurring only in word final. Indicate location of examples in the Reference column. These morphemes are first order. (3) In the second numbered column, list in other successive rows farther down the page, any morpheme(s) occurring (a) in semi-final (i.e., immediately preceding morphemes of the first order) or (b) in both word final and semi-final. Indicate location of examples in the Reference column. Such morphemes are second order. (4) In the third numbered column list any morphemes (a) immediately preceding morphemes of the second order, or (b) immediately preceding second order morphemes in some words and immediately preceding the stem and/or first order morphemes in other words. Indicate in the Reference column the location of examples. These morphemes are third order. (5) Continue in this manner until all suffixes are accounted for in the group of words.

Your chart will look somewhat as follows:

5	4	3	2	1	Reference
				-ik	p. 31 l. 14
			-I		p. 19 l. 8
		-n			p. 12 l. 10
		-man			p. 20 l. 9
		-l			p. 19 l. 7
	-opo				p. 1 l. 1
	-are				p. 35 l. 4
-t					p. 12 l. 6

9.6.5. Compare the scheme obtained in 9.6.2. with that obtained in 9.6.4. Do the charts differ at one or more points?

Would some sort of compromise between the two charts be possible? Thus, granted ten relative orders of suffixes which have been plotted 'fore and aft" according to 9.6.2. and 9.6.4. there may be a given suffix which occurs in third order reckoning from the stem but in fifth order reckoning backwards from word final. Numbering the orders ABSOLUTELY from left to right on both charts we can say that this morpheme occurs no earlier than order 3 and no later than order 6. The distributional data permit it, therefore, to be assigned to any relative order 3-6. On inspection, it may turn out that the morpheme in question appears to be aspectual in meaning and that aspectual morphemes characterize order 5 but no other order. On this basis, then, the morpheme in question may be assigned to order 5. Note that in so assigning this morpheme to order 5 we are not setting up a new tagmeme on the basis of meaning similarity but are using meaning-function similarity to settle a distributional indeterminacy in regard to assignment of a morpheme to a previously identified tagmeme. This procedure is similar to that suggested for clause structure under 3.0.3. where it is suggested that "an item may have been charted in one column which on further analysis more probably belongs in an adjoining column."

9.6.6. Repeat procedures 9.6.2.-5. for prefixes (if present). Note that 9.6.2. would have as its parallel the charting of prefixes from the stem backwards toward word initial, while 9.6.4. would have as its parallel a charting from word initial towards the stem.

9.6.7. As you chart, look for evidence of two or more structurally distinct levels within the word. Thus, Cashibo verbs are (Olive Shell, 1957) not simple stem-affix strings but are built on a BASE which in turn is built on a CORE which is built on a ROOT. Amuesha verbs (Mary Ruth Wise) present an even more extreme example in that they apparently are characterized by six relative levels of structure. A more common sort of situation is the frequently encountered distinction between derivational patterns occurring on a level which we may call the STEM in contrast to inflectional patterns occurring on the WORD level proper.

Evidence for more than one structural level within the word may be of the following sort: (1) Difference in internal organization of one part of the word as opposed to the rest of its structure. Thus, in Zoque and in many languages, stems are successively layered structures to which immediate constituent analysis is readily applicable, while words are stem-affix strings to which immediate constituent analysis is not readily applicable. In Cashibo, the core level is characterized by types of formation (root + root, root + derivative affix) much like we are accustomed to labeling derivation, while base is a core-suffix string with suffixes which group into three groups of which groups A and C contain some three or four morphemes each while group B contains about a dozen relative orders exhibiting some freedom of mutual ordering. The verb proper is a base-suffix string with suffixes of different function from those found in the base. (2) Difference in number and type of constituent tagmemes. This has already been anticipated under the above point (note Cashibo core-base-verb distinction). Derivative affixes manifesting tagmemes of a stem often occur in very varied and restricted patterns. They typically lead to analytical difficulties concerning fossilized versus active patterns. On the contrary, inflectional suffixes of the word proper are usually clearly productive at the present stage of the language. (3) There may be successive evidence of closure as in Amuesha where suffix order 2000 "closes" a construction which then takes further suffixes. Each occurrence of a suffix of this order marks closure of some structural level –whether root, core, base, stem, theme, or word proper. (4) In general, one may simply test the feasibility of distinguishing a further structural level or levels within the word and see if such a distinction clears up difficulties (or gratuitously increases complexity).

If two or more contrastive levels of structure are found within the word or within some word type then these levels should be separately analyzed and charted. A stem level where present in a language may be characterized by: (1) patterns of composition as well as affixation; (2) marked immediate constituent layering. Both these features characterize Zoque stem formation. Thus, nonsimple verb stems may consist of two to five morphemes. Not only are certain derivative suffixes involved in formation of nonsimple verb stems but also such compounding as: verb + verb, attributive + verb, and noun + verb. Successive layers of derivation are seen in such a Zoque stem as *cʌmiʔʌy* 'to load': (1) *cʌmi-ʔʌy* 'to load' is a verb stem derived from the noun stem *cʌmi* 'burden' plus a verbalizing suffix. (2) *cʌm-i* is derived from the verb stem *cʌm* 'to bear' plus a nominalizing suffix.

10. ANALYTICAL PROCEDURES FOR WORD TYPES (WORD LEVEL SYNTAGMEMES)

As with clause types and phrase types we require here a two-fold distinction to establish separate word types. In exemplifying the operation of the two-fold distinction on the word level we draw examples from Candoshi verbs as described by Cox – although Cox gives us no information about verb stems which manifest an obligatory tagmeme in all verb types. The presence and role of the stem is therefore ignored in the Candoshi examples in 10.1.-10.4. below.

10.1. Separate as different word types any two varieties having at least a difference of two in their number of obligatory tagmemes (e.g. one obligatory tagmeme versus three; two obligatory tagmemes versus four). On comparing Candoshi dependent conditional verbs with independent imperative verbs it is immediately evident that the two types of verbs are syntagmemically distinct. Dependent conditional verbs have three obligatory suffixal tagmemes while independent imperative verbs have but one obligatory suffixal tagmeme (Cox's order +2020 consisting of two morphemes *-ŋki* 'imperative' and *-šini* 'imperative with motion' which are found in no other verb type).

10.2. Separate as different word types any two varieties having a difference of one in the number of obligatory tagmemes, provided that a second structural difference is present as well.

Comparison of Candoshi dependent conditional with independent indicative verbs (which have two obligatory suffixal tagmemes) requires a more careful evaluation. The three obligatory suffixal

tagmemes in dependent conditional are: +4200 (morphemes marking person and number of subject), +4510 (one morpheme -*o*
'conditional'), and +(±4540 ±4530 ±4520). The two obligatory
suffixal tagmemes in independent indicative verbs are: +200 (same
morphemes as 4200 of dependent conditional) and +(±540 ±530
±520 ±510). The first three of the latter four tagmemes (at least
one of which must be present in any independent indicative verb)
are identical with 4550-4520 in dependent conditional verbs except
that 4530 involves but one of four morphemes found in 530. Tagmeme 510, (511 -*ša* '2nd order', 512 -*masi* 'first order') has nothing
in common with +4510 (-*o* 'conditional') of the dependent conditional. From the foregoing we deduce one clearly relevant difference between the dependent conditional and the independent indicative, viz. the presence of obligatory 510 in the former, versus its
absence in the latter. Of less clear status but probably relevant
are the differences in the +(540-510) line-up of independent indicative suffixes with the +(4540-4520) line-up of dependent conditional suffixes. But other differences of assured relevance are not
hard to find. Thus, an optional tagmeme ±4400 (-*vii* 'specific')
occurs in the dependent conditional but not in the independent indicative, while another optional tagmeme ±100 (111 -*ya* 'emphatic',
112 -*pa* 'potential', 113 -*ši* 'negative', and 114 -*a* 'interrogative')
occurs in independent indicative but not in the dependent conditional. These features are contrasted in the diagram below (in
which are also included the other optional tagmemes found in these
verb types but not relevant to the above discussion):

Independent Indicative

±800	±700	±600	+(±540	±530	±520	±510)		±300	+200	±100
			FOUR SUFFIXES			Ø				

Dependent Conditional

±4800	±4700	±4600	+(±4540	±4530	±4520)	+4510	±4400	±4300	+4200
			ONE OF THE FOUR			DISTINCTIVE			Ø

The two Candoshi verb types charted above each have ten relative orders of suffixes. By comparison, other Candoshi verb types are considerably simpler structures. Of these simpler structures, Candoshi independent desiderative verbs may be compared with the independent imperative verbs already mentioned. The former have four relative orders of suffixes two of which are obligatory; the latter have three relative orders of suffixes one of which is obligatory. By counting only the number of obligatory suffixal tagmemes in each type it is evident that at least one structural difference separates the two types. Actually, however, closer scrutiny turns up two solid differences here in that (1) +1010 desiderative morphemes peculiar to independent desiderative verbs contrast with +2020 (imperative morphemes) peculiar to independent imperative verbs; while (2) +1200 (same pronoun series occurring as +200 and +4200 above) found in independent desiderative verbs contrasts with its absence in independent imperative verbs. The case for separating the two types is even further strengthened when we note that the two further optional orders found in each type are absent from the other type. In brief, in spite of the drastic restriction in suffixation in both these verb types, neither one shows a single suffixal tagmeme in common with the other. These contrasts are charted below:

Independent Desiderative

+1010		±1300	+1200	±1110
D E S I D E R A T I V E	S U F F I X E S	one suffix 1311 (same as 311)	pronominal suffixes (same as 200 and 4200)	one suffix 1111 (same as 111)

Independent Imperative

+2020		±2510	±2010
I M P E R A T I V E	S U F F I X E S	one suffix 2512 (same as 512)	distinctive suffixes not found elsewhere

The Candoshi data also illustrate a situation which would impel us to seek a further structural difference even granting a different number of obligatory orders. This situation may be symbolized as follows:

$+X \pm Y$ versus $+X +Y$, i.e. one obligatory tagmeme (X) is the same across putative word types which contain a further tagmeme (Y) optional in the one but obligatory in the other. Thus in the independent optative the suffixes are: (a) either $+3011$ (-nta '1st person objective') ± 3112 or (b) $+3012$ (-inč '2nd person objective')

+3112. This gives us one obligatory tagmeme in (a) versus two obligatory tagmemes in (b). Nevertheless this in itself does not determine two contrasting word types since no further structural difference occurs. We have then but two etic variants of the same emic word type.

10.3. Separate as different word types a suspect type containing but one obligatory tagmeme from another suspect type that contains but one obligatory tagmeme provided the two obligatory tagmemes are structurally distinct and a further structural difference is present. Candoshi independent imperative verbs versus independent optative verbs exemplify this fairly well except for the presence of the etic subtype involving +3012 +3112 as just described above. Thus, the Candoshi independent imperative has +2020 which consists of two imperative suffixes while the independent optative has +3010 (varying with +3012 +3110). This difference in the obligatory tagmemes correlates with a further difference in the selection of optional tagmemes. The two verb types in fact share no tagmemes, obligatory or optional. Compare the following chart of independent optative verb suffixes with the chart for independent imperative given above:

Independent Optative

±3700-3500	+3010	+/±3110
(a composite order: cf. 711, 542, 521 of Independent Indicative)	Object suffixes	one suffix (same as 112)

10.4. For a pair of suspect word types each with two obligatory tagmemes, separate as different types whenever (a) both obligatory tagmemes of one differ from both obligatory tagmemes of the other, or (b) but one pair of tagmemes differs and a further structural difference may be found. We may symbolize situation (a) as XY versus QR; and situation (b) as XY versus XZ. In the latter case we look for a further structural difference. Thus both Candoshi independent indicative verbs and independent desiderative have an obligatory order consisting of the same series of personal pronoun endings (+200 in independent indicative; +1200 in independent desiderative). The independent indicative has +(540-10) while the independent desiderative has +1010. This latter distinction gives us one structural difference. A second difference is seen in the drastic restriction on occurrence of optional tagmas in the independent desiderative where only two such orders are found as compared with five in the independent indicative.

10.5. Generalize the above (10.4.) for any two suspect varieties of word containing the same number of obligatory tagmas of a number three or higher.

10.6. Join any two varieties of word not separable by a dual structural contrast into one word type with etic variants – unless strong analogical pressures make a separation feasible.

Thus, Pike ("Dimensions of Grammatical Constructions", *Language* 38.238-9) restates an aspect of Tzotzil verb structure as presented by Delgaty. In Pike's restatement he brings together in one type hortatory and imperative verbs that had been presented separately by Delgaty. Pike observes: "In Tzotzil we find an elaborate differentiation of alloconstructions which are caused by the particular pronominal affix used in the verb. ... Once it is clear that the Tzotzil system allows substantial differences in alloconstructions due to personal pronouns, the way seems to me to be open, by somewhat parallel analysis, to unite into a single emic construction his substantially different hortatory and imperative clauses". Pike here says "clause" rather than "verb" – but seems obviously to be dealing with the latter rather than with the former.)

10.7. Arrange partially similar and systematically contrasting word types in one or more matrices with appropriate dimensions.

Thus Pike suggests the following matrix for Cashibo verbs: A transitive-intransitive dichotomy (depending on the structure of the

base) constitutes the horizontal dimension while various categories
of principal and subordinate (depending on the pattern of affixation
in the margin of the verb proper) constitute the vertical dimension:

Principal	Transitive	Intransitive
Personal	X	X
Imperative	X	X
Purposive	X	X
Subordinate With inflectional concord to transitive principal verb	X	X
With inflectional concord to intransitive principal verb	X	X

10.8. Inspect the posited matrix or matrices for (a) confirmation of types posited; and (b) clues as to possible
types yet uncatalogued (by observing lacunae in a matrix).

11. ANALYTICAL PROCEDURES FOR WORD LEVEL TAGMEMES

11.0.1. List exhaustively morphemes and morpheme
clusters in each tentatively identified function slot (tagma). If there is a slot in which otherwise free forms belonging to
open classes may occur, exemplify this with a variety of examples.

11.0.2. Attempt to give a functional label to each slot
(stem, aspect, tense, person, number, gender, diminutive, etc.).

11.1. In many languages the relative orders of affixes
carefully plotted prove to be significant function-sets,
i.e. (word level) tagmemes. However, several possible trouble
spots are described in this section.

11.2. Look for pairs of word level tagmas that are suspect of being the same tagmeme in that they are similar as
to functions of manifesting items and are mutually exclusive in distribution.

11.2.1. Look first for such suspect pairs between relative orders of prefixes or of suffixes in the same word type. For example, in the prefixes of the Apachean verb there is an iterative mode prefix in order 5 and other modal prefixes in order 11; while there are deictic subject prefixes in order 8 and other subject prefixes in order 12. Orders 5 and 11 are mutually exclusive in the same verb as are also 8 and 12. We therefore set up here two suspect pairs of word level tagmas: 5, 11 and 8, 12.

11.2.2. Look for suspect pairs composed of a relative order of prefixes mutually exclusive with a relative order of suffixes. Thus, in Choctaw, most affixes marking subject of transitive verbs occur as 2nd order prefixes (reckoning from the stem). There is, however, one lone suffix -li 'I' which marks first person singular. Here the first order suffix -li and the second order prefixes constitute a pair of suspect tagmas.

Again, at one point in the Cebuano paradigm of goal focus verbs, two modes are marked by suffixes: -un nonfactive and -a privative. But a further mode, the factive, is marked by gi- (Flores, p. 64). The tagma manifested by suffixes and the tagma manifested by a prefix constitute a suspect pair.

11.3. Any such mutually exclusive suspect pair as posited in the above two procedures will prove to manifest the same word level tagmeme unless it should prove that the two mutually exclusive tagmemes are identifying contrastive features which belong to structurally contrastive types. Thus, for example, if in the Apachean verb prefixes the iterative prefix in order 5 proves to determine a structurally different word string from that selecting any of the other mode prefixes in order 11, then orders 5 and 11 do not constitute the same tagmeme, but rather manifest different tagmemes distributed in different strings. The decision as to whether Apachean verbs containing order 5 are structurally distinct from Apachean verbs containing order 11 must be made on the basis of absence or presence of a second structural difference correlating with choice of order 5 versus order 11.

11.4. Inspect the data for morpheme clusters suspect

of manifesting but one word level tagmeme. Thus, Cashibo has two suffixes *-biá* ~ *-kiá* 'while going' and *-bĭcĭ* ~ *-k*ʷ*acĭ* 'coming' which occur among the base-forming suffixes of group B (Shell 189, and 191). Either morpheme may be preceded by *-oko* 'haltingly, stopping and starting', which occurs only in this environment preceding the 'going' and 'coming' morphemes.

11.5. Inspect the data for mutual dependence of prefix and suffix (two tagmas suspect of being one discontinuous tagmeme bracketing the stem).

This seems to characterize pronominal markers of subject affixed to the Hebrew verb. Thus, in the so-called "perfect" or "sufformative" tense of Biblical Hebrew, suffixes mark the following person-number distinctions in the singular: 3m., 3f., 2m., 2f., 1c. (common gender); and in the plural: 3c., 2m., 2f., 1c. But in the "imperfect" or "preformative" tense there is an interplay of prefix with suffix to express similar distinctions:

3 m.s.	y-		3 m.pl.	y-...-u
3 f.s.	t-		3 f.pl.	t-...-nɔ
2 m.s.	t-		2 m.pl.	t-...-u
2 f.s.	t-...-i		2 f.pl.	t-...-nɔ
1 c.s.	ʔ-		1 c.pl.	n-

11.6. Recognize the morpheme cluster (11.4.) and the discontinuous prefix-suffix sequence (11.5.) as each constituting one word level tagmeme when over-all tactical simplicity and structural parallelism make such a decision feasible. Thus, in recognizing the Cashibo clusters *-okobiá*, *-okokiá*, *-okobĭcĭ*, and *-okok*ʷ*acĭ* as clusters manifesting but one word level Cashibo tagmeme (actually on the structural level of the base within the word), Shell avoids setting up a further order of affixes manifested only by *-oko* and dependent on the occurrence of *-biá*, *-kiá*, *-bĭcĭ*, or *-k*ʷ*acĭ* in the following order. In view of the peculiar fact that Cashibo affixes of Group B have a certain freedom of mutual ordering, the en bloque movement of *-okobiá*, etc. is no doubt a further reason for considering these morpheme clusters to manifest but one word level tagmeme.

In regard to the Hebrew prefix-suffix dependency we can, of course, set up separate prefixal and suffixal tagmemes for the imperfect tense: PNG' (prefixal person-number-gender tagmeme) with four morphemes: *y-* 3 m., *ʔ-* 1 c.sg., *n-* 1 c.pl., and *t-* other person-number-gender combinations; and PNG" (suffixal person-number-gender tagmeme: *-i* 2 f.s., *-u* 3/2 m.pl., and *-nɔ* 3/2 f.pl. But in that no such person-number-gender groupings of the sort just posited for *t-*, *-u*, and *-nɔ* occur in the other tense of the Hebrew verb, this separate tagmemic analysis of prefix and suffix breaks the parallelism of the two tenses. If, however, we are willing to grant a bracketing tagmeme with discontinuous manifestation, then the two tenses are again parallel as to types of person-number-gender distinctions made.

11.7. Inspect the data to see if some confusion in relative orders of affixes may be due to a limited freedom of position of occurrence on the part of certain orders of affixes. In Cashibo a striking example of this occurs. Cashibo base-forming suffixes fall into three groups with group A occurring next to the core, and with group C occurring final in the base. Suffixes of these two groups behave as affixes normally behave, i.e., they occur distributed in relative orders. But the dozen optional orders of suffixes in group B (which follows group A and precedes group C) misbehave quite badly, i.e. "its members show great flexibility as to position" (Shell 193). Specifically, certain pairs of group B suffixes may change positions with each other.

If a certain freedom of occurrence is found to characterize one part of a stem-affix string, then the privileges of occurrence of the affixes which display this freedom should be analyzed and charted (cf. Shell chart 3 c, p. 196).

12. CONCLUDING PROCEDURES FOR WORD LEVEL ANALYSIS

12.1. Any residues by-passed during earlier stages of analysis should now be considered.

12.2. Write a summary description of word level syntagmemes (word types) and tagmemes. Include appropriate charts and formulae.

12.3. Check this description against a larger corpus (text material, further elicitation, forms overheard in speech of native speakers).

12.4. Revise the description to account for the fuller corpus. Write up in more complete and elegant form.

IV

SENTENCE LEVEL PROCEDURES

13. PRELIMINARY PROCEDURES FOR SENTENCE ANALYSIS

In analyzing sentence structure it is especially important to rely upon text material rather than on elicited material – in that the very process of elicitation may cause distortion (following of the word order or general syntactic mold dictated by the investigator's question – especially if he elicits in one language forms in another). Sentences overheard in actual conversation are, of course, of equal value with sentences found in text material. The informant-analyst is able to produce sentences at will to aid his analysis. He must beware, however, of letting his analysis be marred by (a) preoccupation with highly unusual or marginal forms (which would possibly be challenged as strained or unnatural by another informant); or (b) letting his emerging views of sentence structure dictate what he chooses to note or ignore. In view of these difficulties, even the informant-analyst may find it useful to resort to a recorded corpus.

13.0. Definition of sentence: a class of syntagmemes of a hierarchical order ranking above such syntagmemes as the clause and below such syntagmemes as the paragraph and discourse. It may consist of a single clause, of a patterned combination of clauses, or of a clause fragment (usually of phrasal structure and often dependent in sense on other sentences in the linguistic context or on context of situation). It tends to be characterized by more closure and grammatical independence than the clause, as evidenced by introducing and closing particles as well as by features of intonation and pause. Affirmation, quotation, conditional propositions, balance, antithesis, and chronological or logical sequence (and sometimes question and command) are meanings often expressed by sentence structures.

13.1. Isolate sentence units in the corpus by drawing

bars at sentence boundaries. Bracket sequences which seem to be too difficult for initial handling. These bracketed sequences constitute a residue which should be considered later under 16.

In isolating sentences in connected text we may need to take into account such features as (1) distribution of conjunctions and/or closing particles; and (2) distribution of intonation, pause, and allied features. But we also will consider as relevant: (3) ANY PATTERNED DEPENDENCY which is (a) below the paragraph and/or discourse, and (b) involves combinations of clauses not having the overall structure of single clauses. These three points are discussed in detail below.

(1) In some languages which use conjunctions with frequency, the incidence of certain types of conjunctions may mark sentence boundary. In Trique, e.g. occurrence of one of the following two conjunctions marks onset of sentence: za^3ni^4 'but', $da^3d\underline{i}^{35}P$ zi^4 'because'; while ni^4 'and', nga^{43} ni^4 'and then', da^3P nga^4 zi^3 'then also', also mark sentence onset provided a subordinate conjunction does not introduce the preceding clause. In other languages (e.g. English) conjunctions serve to mark union of clauses within sentences while absence of conjunction more regularly marks sentence boundary.

(2) Pause may correlate frequently enough with the boundary between two grammatical sentences to be a valuable clue especially in early stages of analysis. Furthermore, a given type of pause may prove to be an identifying-contrastive feature of a sentence type in a given language. But in that the phonological sentence and grammatical sentence do not necessarily coincide one should beware of joining two otherwise independent sentences into one grammatical sentence solely because they constitute one unified phonological unit unbroken by pause. Thus the English *I came, I saw, I conquered* (and presumably the Latin original *veni vidi vici*) may be pronounced as one intonation and pause group.[1] But this need not

[1] With either of the following intonation patterns the sequence in question would be one phonological sentence (The system of symbolizing English intonation is Pike's):

	I came	*I saw*	*I conquered*
	3 – °2	2 – °2	2 – °2 – 4
	3 – °2	3 – °2	3 – °2 – 4

of itself prove that the sequence is one grammatical sentence as well. In fact, confusion of grammatical and phonological sentence may be at the source of much of the confusion regarding "What is a sentence?" in English (cf. Fries, *The Structure of English* 9-28).

Using intonation and pause as clues, one should look about for other formal features witnessing to the possible grammatical unity of the sequence. In Trique about eighty to ninety per cent of the sentence boundaries (marked quite regularly by conjunctions) are marked also by pause; but some rather marked pauses occur internally in sentences and occasionally two rather short sentences are united in the same pause group.

Consistent absence of pause may be a clue that a sentence boundary is not present. In Trique one level of sentence structure consists of paratactic union of two clauses in patterned combination without intervening conjunction or pause. A speaker who needs to pause for breath will pause somewhere within one of the paired clauses rather than at the seam of the two clauses.

(3) Patterned dependency characterizes any linguistic structure on whatever level. A patterned dependency is a span characterized by internal restriction so that the structure of the parts is partially dependent on the structure of the whole. Within a patterned dependency there is less choice than at the boundary between two such spans. As such a patterned dependency, the sentence is intermediate between the clause on the one hand and the paragraph and/or discourse on the other hand. In that paragraph and discourse are also patterned dependencies, we cannot define sentence as any patterned dependency bigger than one clause.

A further reason for not so defining the sentence is that a clause may include another clause within itself as a manifestation of some clause level tagmeme: e.g., in *I came before you arrived*, the clause *before you arrived* manifests clause level temporal tagmeme. As such it is commutable with such expressions as *yesterday*, and *an hour ago*. Now the entire expression *I came before you arrived* is certainly an English sentence but not on the ground that it is a combination of two clauses. Rather, it is an English sentence on the same grounds that *I came yesterday* is an English sentence.

Whether temporal tagmeme in the *I came...* frame is manifested by a noun phrase or by a subordinate clause, the resulting sequence has the structure of a one-clause sentence. For a minimal sentence may consist of a single clause, even as a minimal clause may consist of a phrase, and a minimal phrase may consist of a single word.

There are other English sequences, however, which clearly involve combinations of clauses not capable of explanation as clause-within-clause: *If he should be the cause of it let me know. John went downtown, but Bill stayed home.*

As a patterned dependency involving two or more clauses not having the overall structure of a single clause, the internal unity of a sentence type may be marked by such features as: (1) restriction as to the selection of component clause types, (2) restriction as to the sequence of tenses, aspects, modes, or persons in predicates of component clause, (3) other restrictions in internal structure of component clauses, (4) required linear ordering of component clauses, (5) sharing of some noun phrase in simultaneous dual syntactic function in two component clauses. The first four features are summarily mentioned here but are discussed and illustrated below in 14. and 15.; the fifth was first mentioned by Hockett in reference to Potawatomi (where he terms the phenomenon PIVOTING):

Pɛ-jɛ-pməpt·ot   Po   Pɛs·pən   Pɛ-ki-wapmat   Pamon
'he-ran-along   the   raccoon   he-saw   a beehive
Pɛ-kočnənət
it-hung-down.'

i.e., 'As the coon ran along he saw a beehive hanging down'. In this sentence *Po Pɛs·pən* 'the raccoon' functions as subject of the preceding verb *Pɛ-jɛ-pməpt·ot* 'he ran along' and of the following verb *Pɛ-ki-wapmat* 'he saw'. Similarly, *Pamon* 'beehive' functions as object of *Pɛ-ki-wapmat* 'he saw' and subject of *Pɛ-kočnənət* 'it-hung-down'. The entire sentence is tightly bound grammatically by the occurrence of these two syntactically ambivalent nouns at the seams of the component clauses.

Sentences involving combinations of clauses may range from closely-knit structures which could be described as expanded clauses

to loosely-knit structures that are, in effect, small paragraphs.[2] Two
sentence types in Zoque afford an interesting contrast here: (1) The
closely-knit sequence sentence consists of two or three clauses in
parataxis but resembles the structure of a single clause in that not
only may two clauses share a syntactically ambivalent noun (as in
Potawatomi above) but a common peripheral (e.g., clause expressing purpose, cause, or temporal) may orbit around the clauses in
parataxis. The actors or subjects of the clauses have the same
referent.

henemete wʌ?ahu?kam   maŋbam   tiyʌhkahe   maŋbam
'Then   when-it's-good it's-going-to what-you-call-it it's-going-to
kor·ecʌk te nʌ   ?ihtu?kam seis dias
run   the juice when-it-has six days'.

'Then, after six days, when it's good, the juice will what-you-call-it,
will ferment'.

In the preceding sentence the paired clauses *maŋbam tiyukahe*
'it's-going-to what-you-call-it' and *maŋbam kor·ecʌk te nʌ* 'the juice
is going to run' constitute the nucleus of the sentence, while temporal clauses modifying the nucleus are preposed and postposed.
(2) In contrast the Zoque loosely-knit sequence sentence: (a) has
neither syntactically ambivalent nouns nor common peripherals;
furthermore (b), the actors or subjects may be dissimilar. It is the
absence of conjunction (internally) and final pause that indicate the
unity of this rambling unit which resembles a short paragraph:

i   te mula?s mapa   čumbuhtyahe eyatite   mapa
and   the mules going-to carry-it-out in-another-way going-to
nʌyos mule ar·ieru?s
work mules arrieros'

'And the mules are going to carry it out; in another way the arrieros
are going to work the mules.' This sentence starts with *i* 'and',
which is a conjunction often initiating Zoque sentences.

[2] Harwood Hess, in his unpublished study of Otomi grammar, describes a
situation in which 'sentence' is a unit sufficiently long and complex to be more
on the order of what we are accustomed to consider a paragraph.

To this point our discussion of sentence has been restricted to structures consisting of a single clause or of a combination of clauses. Languages usually contain several sentence types nonclausal in structure. Thus, in English we find: exclamations (*Fine!, Oh!, No!, Nuts!*), vocatives (*Mary!, John!*), greetings (*Hi, Howdy*), short questions (*Who?, Which one?, Why?*), and answers to questions (*Alexander Brown. The green one. Roses and marigolds*).

13.2. Copy each tentatively isolated sentence onto a 4 × 6 filing slip with translation (if the latter is necessary for your handling of the data) and accurate reference to location in your corpus. Enough examples of one clause and nonclausal sentences should be filed to assure the analyst that he has a valid sampling of such structures. Combinations of clauses involving some length and complexity require the filing of a considerable volume of examples before an adequate corpus is obtained.

13.3. Sort the slips impressionistically into groups which seem to differ structurally from each other. Nonclausal sentences can be sorted into one group with possible further division. One clause sentences may be classified into such groups as: declarative, interrogative, imperative, negative (unless such distinctions have been given structural status on the clause level).

Multiple clause sentences not structured as clause-within-clause present greater problems in initial grouping. An initial grouping can sometimes be made by separating sentences composed of clauses joined by conjunction from those composed of clauses joined in parataxis without conjunction. These two large groups can then be subdivided in various ways scarcely possible to illustrate without resort to a given language. Quotations of one or more sorts, conditional sentences of one or more sorts, and various sorts of circumstance-event, antecedent-consequent, and effect-cause combinations often prove relevant.

13.4. For each group attempt to work out a summary distributional scheme in which the relations of the various elements of the sentence are symbolized. The very attempt to work out such summary distributional schemes may suggest further divisions of groups already made, combination of groups posited on inadequate grounds, and reshuffling of examples from group to group.

The internal structure of component clauses is not relevant as such to sentence structure. But any feature of the structure of a component clause may prove to be relevant. We are not, therefore, concerned here with plotting such strings as predicate-subject-object-location, etc., but rather structures of which clauses, phrases, conjunctions, particles, intonational contours, and pauses are possible elements. Nevertheless, any part of any element may prove to be significant in the patterning of the sentence. A few sample schemes (cf. Introduction: Symbols and Rewrite Operations) follow:

TRIQUE INDIRECT QUOTATION SENTENCE

1. +BQ +Quotative +Quoted ±EQ.
2. +BQ (beginning of quote): short clause involving ta^3h 'say', ga^3ni^{23} ru^3wa^{23} 'think', or a few other verbs.
3. Quotative: zi^3zi^4 'that, to the effect that'
4. +Quoted: almost any possible sentence of moderate length (more restricted range of quoted than in a direct quotation sentence).
5. ±EQ (end of quote): same as BQ except that the clause may be introduced by (we^2) da^3h 'thus' (e.g. 'said he').

$ta^{34}h$ ne^3h zi^3h zi^3zi^4 nu^3 $ni^3\textrm{?}i^2$ $re^5\textrm{?}$ / we^2 da^3h $ta^{34}h$ ne^3h zi^3h
'say they   that not know you,   so say they'
'They say that you don't know.'

ISTHMUS ZAPOTEC YES-OR-NO INTERROGATIVE SENTENCE

(Pickett pp. 20-21)
1. ±QI ±Margin +SB +Yes-or-no closer.
2. ±QI (question introducer): ⌐nyé?e.
3. ±Margin: 'if' clause.
4. +SB (sentence base): declarative independent clause.
5. +Yes-or-no closer: *lá*.

'nyéʔe 'če   úʔ lugi'aʔa lá

"?   going you market ?'

'Are you or aren't you going to market?'

ZOQUE CONTRARY TO FACT CONDITIONAL SENTENCE

1. ±Pr +Ap

2. ±Pr (protasis): clause which includes (T: *naʔŋ* 'past') and is introduced by *hoʔka* 'if' or *ke tal* 'what if'. Pr is omitted only with sufficient context.

3. +Ap (apodosis): clause which contains (T: *naʔŋ* 'past')

hoʔka išahpa-naʔŋ   tuhyahpa-naʔŋ

'if   they-him-saw-had they-him-shot-had'

'If they had seen him they would have shot him.'

13.5. Inspect the sentence schemes for possible evidence of two or more contrasting levels of sentence structure. While it is desirable to accommodate the data within the simplest possible framework, in some languages there is a distinct level intermediate between clause and sentence. In both Trique and Chatino such a level has been posited and termed the COLON level. Trique colons are distinct from sentences in that: (a) Colons are composed of a pair of clauses (or rarely, three clauses) paratactically combined without conjunction and (in most cases) without pause. Phonologically, the unity of the colon is greater than that of the sentence. (b) Lexically, there is often considerable co-occurrence restriction between the two verbs manifesting predicate in the two parts of the colon. (c) Grammatically, there are often peculiar restrictions on the internal structure of a clause manifesting one part of a colon. (d) Certain colons may share noun phrases in ambivalent functions (13.1.). By contrast, Trique sentence structures are less compact, are put together with conjunctions, permit pauses at important internal seams, and do not have such overt marks of unity as the syntactically ambivalent noun phrases which occur at the seams of certain colon types. Furthermore, Trique colons often manifest sentence level tagmemes in a manner similar to that in which phrases manifest clause level tagmemes, or words manifest phrase level tagmemes.

By contrast, while Zoque has a contrast between closely-knit and loosely-knit sequence sentences (see 13.1.) that parallels the contrast between colon and sentence in Trique and Chatino, nevertheless, this distinction seems of value chiefly in distinguishing the two sentence types. Separate levels of sentence structure need not (and should not) be posited unless such a distinction proves to be of general relevance. In Trique, e.g. where there are fourteen structurally contrastive colon types and at least fifteen structurally contrastive sentence types, the colon versus sentence distinction is of considerable relevance.

Examples of Trique and Chatino colons are included at various points in the following procedures. Such examples are relevant to the analysis of sentence structure whether or not a given language distinguishes two levels in this general area of its structure.

14. ANALYTICAL PROCEDURES FOR SENTENCE TYPES

In separating or joining two similar but suspect sentence types our criterion is the same as that employed on lower structural levels, i.e. insistence on a dual structural difference. The application of this criterion is, however, more subtle and varied than on lower levels. This is resultant on the fact that the sentence level is a relatively high hierarchical level. Of possible relevance therefore are (1) any feature of the internal structure of any syntagmeme manifesting any sentence level tagmeme; and (2) any sequence restriction between such features. Such features as absence versus presence of a given tagmeme and obligatory versus optional status continue to be relevant.

In many European languages tense sequence between clauses is an important feature. In Trique, while sequence of aspect-mood is important in distinguishing some sentence types, other sequence restrictions involve (a) types of clauses which may follow each other; (b) same versus different referents of actors in the clauses, (c) same versus different verbs in the clauses. In counting structural differences a sequence restriction can probably be considered to constitute but one structural difference although affecting both of two paired clauses. Other relevant factors already mentioned are (1) distribution of intonation contours and pauses; (2) distribution of conjunctions and particles; (3) distribution of functionally ambivalent nouns. Last but by no means least, the transform potential (or derivation) of one sentence type versus another may be a very direct witness to differing structures.

In Highland New Guinea languages such as Tairora one very important sequence restriction is that one type of verb, the medial verb, occurs in nonfinal clauses; while another type of verb, the final verb, occurs in sentence-final clauses. Medial verbs are in general more restricted in affixation than final verbs. Medial verbs are, however, marked by a peculiar order of affixes not found in final verbs – affixes the function of which is to anticipate the person of the actor of the following verb should that actor not be the same person as the actor of the medial verb.

14.1. Separate any two varieties of sentences which have at least a difference of two in the number of obligatory tagmemes.

Thus, Trique monologue sequence sentence B is seen to be distinct from the comparison sentence. The former has but one obligatory tagmeme (with two preposed optional tagmemes):

$\pm$ temporal margin $\pm$ sentence conjunction$_1$ + sentence base as in $a^5\mathcal{P}$ $gq^3\mathcal{P}q^{34}h$ zi^3 (sentence base) 'already went off he'. ni^4 $a^5\mathcal{P}$ $gq^3\mathcal{P}q^{34}h$ zi^3 (sentence conjunction$_1$, sentence base) 'and he already went off'. nga^{43} $gu^3\check{z}u^3mq^2h$ ni^4 $a^5\mathcal{P}$ $gq^3\mathcal{P}q^{34}h$ zi^3 (temporal margin, sentence conjunction$_1$, sentence base) 'when I came (and) he already had gone off'. The comparison sentence has three obligatory tagmemes:

+ Comparison + Type + Antitype:

$ro^2\mathcal{P}$ $gi^3\mathcal{P}ya^{21}$ $re^5\mathcal{P}$ we^2 da^3h $gi^3\mathcal{P}ya^{32}$ 'like did you just so did-I' (comparison: $ro^2\mathcal{P}$ 'like'; type: $gi^3\mathcal{P}ya^{21}$ $re^5\mathcal{P}$ 'did you'; antitype: we^2 da^3h $gi^3\mathcal{P}ya^{23}$ 'just so did-I').

14.2. Separate any two varieties of sentence which have a difference of one in the number of obligatory tagmemes provided that a further structural difference is present somewhere.

On this basis a sentence type of nonclausal structure or composed of a clause fragment is separable from a sentence type consisting of two obligatory tagmemes manifested by clauses. Formulaically represented, the contrast may be seen as follows: Z ('Not yet') versus QR ('If he is sick. I'll not go'). QR, as a conditional sentence type, has two obligatory tagmemes, while Z has but one tagmeme manifested by a clause fragment. Furthermore, the clause fragments manifesting Z are distinct from both Q and R which are manifested by clauses. This gives us our second difference.

In Trique two types of particle sentences are distinguishable: Particle A which consists of one tagmeme, $+Pr_1$: $m^2?m^5$ 'no', m^{53} 'yes'; and Particle B which consists of two obligatory tagmemes, $+Pr_2$: other particles or particle expressions $+Voc$: kinship terms used in address (e.g. mq^{34} di^3ni^2 'hello, brother' and da^3h $ga^5?$ / di^3ni^2 'that's all, brother'). In contrasting these two sentence types we note that Particle A has but one obligatory tagmeme while Particle B has two obligatory tagmemes. Furthermore, Pr_1 is distinct from Pr_2 in that Pr_1 is manifested by a very limited class of gesture-like interjections of peculiar phonological structure (syllabic m occurs nowhere else in Trique). Furthermore, Pr_1 may not have phrasal expansion while Pr_2 may.

In the Chontal of Oaxaca, intonation contours serve as identifying contrastive features of sentence types. Affirmative and interrogative (Yes or no) sentences are distinguished by (1) differing intonation patterns; and (2) optional presence of a *tés* interrogative particle in the latter sentence type. Thus, Waterhouse (p. 40) gives the following example:

ñí	kʾata sálʾe Pípa el	xwíx

'The fiesta went well.'

(tés) ñí	kʾata sálʾe Pípa	élxwíx

'Did the fiesta go well?'

14.3. Inspect varieties of sentence which have the same number of obligatory tagmemes. Separate two such varieties of sentence wherever a two-fold difference can be established between them, provided that at least one difference involves the obligatory tagmemes.

In Trique, effect-cause colons and behaviour-purpose colons both have two obligatory tagmemes. The following colon is effect-cause: ni^4 ni^{35} $gwi^3gq^5\text{?}q^3h$ $ga^3ta^{35}\text{?}$ $n\cdot e^{34}$ $ne\text{?}e^3$ ru^3wa^{23} nu^2wi^3 $gi^3\text{?}ya^3h$ dre^3h 'and Thursday afternoon the baby was baptized in the church by the priest'. The effect tagmeme is manifested by the first clause $ni^4...nu^2wi^3$ 'And Thursday afternoon the baby was baptized in the church'. The cause tagmeme is manifested by $gi^3\text{?}ya^3h$ dre^3h 'made/did the priest'. In this colon type: (1) It is required that actor or subject refer to different persons in the two clauses. (2) Occasionally the order of the two tagmemes may be reversed. (3) Effect tagmeme may be manifested by any clause type in Trique – including meteorological clause (clauses of meteorological import: 'dawn', nightfall', 'rain'). A behaviour-purpose colon follows: $a^3k\underline{i}^{21}$ $du^3gwa^3zq^4$ nga^3h $gq^4\text{?}q^4h$ $zi^3na^4\text{?}u^4$ dq^3h 'the town hall of Putla was calling for that man to go'. Behaviour tagmeme is manifested by the clause: $a^3k\underline{i}^{21}$ $du^3gwa^3zq^4$ nga^3h 'the town hall of Putla was calling', while the rest of the colon manifests purpose tagmeme. Unlike the effect-cause colon the behaviour-purpose colon (1) may have same or different actor/subject in both clauses; and (2) neither tagmeme may be manifested by a meteorological clause. But even more diagnostic of a behaviour-purpose colon is the following aspect-mood restriction (which is not characteristic of an effect-cause colon): The verb of the clause manifesting purpose tagmeme must be incremented by the modal suffix (and thus be in the anticipatory mood).

The Zoque direct quotation sentence is distinct from the indirect quotation sentence. Although both sentence types are composed +Quotation formula +Quoted, nevertheless there are the following differences: (1) In a direct quotation, the quotation formula may occur preposed, postposed, or interlarded; in an indirect quotation the quotation formula may occur preposed only. (2) In a direct quotation, the quoted is simply juxtaposed to the quotation formula; in an indirect quotation, the quoted is introduced by *ke* 'that', or *ho?ka* 'to the effect that, that'. (3) In the direct quotation the quoted may be a series of sentences, (in fact a discourse), while in the indirect quotation it has the structure of but a single sentence.[3]

14.4. Inspect varieties of sentence distinguishable by but one overt difference to see if (a) transform is possible in one, but not possible in the other; or (b) one is a transform of a structure of which the other is not. In either events separate as sentence types.

Thus, in Chatino, there two types of colons one of which seems to express situation-result, while the other seems to express activity-instigation. But can the requisite two-fold formal difference be demonstrated to corroborate this alleged semantic distinction? An overt difference is seen in that while unrestricted sequence of aspect is permitted in the activity-instigation colon, there are the following restrictions in the situation-result colon: (a) either the verbs in both clauses are in the same aspect, or (b) the following sequences of aspects occur: (1) completive in clause one, continuative or intentive in clause two; or (2) continuative in clause one and intentive in clause two. This overt difference correlates with a difference in transform potential. While no transform of the situation-result colon is possible, the activity-instigation colon may be transformed to a reason sentence (on a higher level of structure involving use of connectives and particles) as follows: Reverse the clauses of the activity-instigation colon and interpose $ko?^2$ $t\check{s}a?^2$ 'that's why'. Examples of these two colon types follow:

SITUATION-RESULT COLON

$nguhwi^1$ $y?o^1$ $kuwi?^{32}$ (= situation) $yi?u^{32}$ $kuwi?^{32}$ $?i^1$ $ne?^3$
'died   mother baby   lived   baby   of hers'
(= result)
'The baby's mother died but her baby lived.'

ACTIVITY-INSTIGATION COLON

ha^4 ku^{32} no^2 $kuta^{32}$ (= activity) $ndik\acute{i}^1$
'negation will-eat-he thing will-give-you   is-angry-he

---

[3] A sentence may include a paragraph just as a phrase may include a clause; cf· 15.1. (4).

$tiʔ^{32}$ $ʔį^2$ (= instigation)
    to-you'
'He won't eat anything that you give him because he's angry with you.'

The latter may be transformed to a reason sentence as follows: $ndikį^1$ $tiʔ^{32}$ $ʔį^2$ $kǫʔ^2$ $tšaʔ^2$ ha^4 ku^{32} $nǫ^2$ $kuta^{32}$ 'He's angry with you, that's why he won't eat anything you give him.' But to attempt so to transform the former leads to nonsense: 'Her baby lived, that's why the baby's mother died.'

14.5. Join any two varieties of sentence not separated by a dual structural contrast into one sentence type – unless strong analogical pressures require a separation.

Thus, in some languages a sentence which is discourse medial (or paragraph medial) must begin with a conjunction, while the opening sentence of a discourse (or paragraph) does not begin with a conjunction. Unless some additional structural distinction is present this does not give us a two-fold difference and does not determine separate sentence types. Rather, occurrence or non-occurrence of conjunction determines etic varieties of whatever sentence types are involved. This does not deny the relevance of the distinction (sentence beginning with conjunction versus sentence not beginning with conjunction) to the structure of the discourse or paragraph. Units need not be emic on a lower level to be relevant on a higher level. Thus [p] and [pᶜ] may be allophones in a given language but nevertheless of considerable relevance to the setting up of stress groups in that language in that one allophone occurs stress-group initial while another occurs stress-group medial or final.

Trique contrary to fact conditions are not a separate sentence type but a subtype of what we might call the specific conditional sentence (as opposed to a general conditional sentence). As subtypes of the specific conditional sentence type, Trique contrary to fact conditions and noncommittal conditions differ only by presence of a contrary to fact particle in the first clause of the former.

Contrary to fact subtype: zi^3zi^4 $nų^4$ $gq^3ʔq^{34}h$ zi^3 $gu^3kĩ^3$ ni^4 $na^3ri^{34}ʔ$

du³gwi³⁴ʔ zi³ nga⁴ zo²ʔ 'If he had gone yesterday he would have met him' (Implication: but he didn't go yesterday and he didn't meet him.)

Non-committal subtype: *zi³zi⁴ gq³ʔq³⁴h zi³ gu³ki³ ni⁴ na³ri³⁴ʔ du³gwi³⁴ʔ zi³ nga⁴ zo²ʔ* 'If he went yesterday he met him' (Implication: we don't know whether or not he went or whether or not he met him, but if he went he met him).

In the above examples, *zi³zi⁴* is 'if'; *nu⁴* 'contrary to fact' particle; *gq³ʔq³⁴h* 'went'; *zi³* 'he'; *gu³ki³* 'yesterday'; *ni⁴* 'and'; *na³ri³⁴ʔ du³gwi³⁴ʔ* 'met'; *nga⁴* 'with'; *zo²ʔ* 'he, him' (additional third person).

In an unpublished study K. Pride very carefully lists etic varieties of colon structures as co-occurrence subtypes. In the activity-instigation colon she lists seven subtypes (read · as 'co-occurs with', C as 'clause' and K as 'colon'):

$$C_1 C_2 C_{11} C_{13} K_1 \cdot C_{11}$$
$$C_1 C_5 C_{11} K_3 \cdot C_2$$
$$C_1 C_{11} C_{13} K_{12} \cdot C_1$$
$$C_1 K_{12} \cdot C_5$$
$$C_1 C_{13} K_3 \cdot C_3$$
$$C_{13} \cdot K_{11}$$
$$C_1 C_3 \cdot K_4$$

Thus, the first line above tells us that when clause type eleven (that is, the first clause type of clause decade class 10) manifests instigation tagmeme, then clause one, two, eleven, thirteen or colon one may manifest activity tagmeme. Obviously, further data from an enlarged corpus will modify somewhat this picture. Ultimately we are interested in co-occurrence subtypes in the sense of what CAN occur and what CAN NOT occur rather than what happens to manifest a given tagmeme in a given corpus. In that there is reason to believe that subtypes of this nature do characterize colon structures in Trique and Chatino, careful analysis of these subtypes will make the grammars of these languages more practically useful and theoretically defensible.

14.6. Arrange partially similar but systematically contrasting sentence types into one or more matrices with appropriate dimensions.

In Zoque it was noticed that several of the sentence types seemed to form pairs. Thus, there are two types of conditional sentences (general versus contrary to fact), two types of quotations (direct versus indirect), and two types of sequence sentences (closely-knit versus loosely-knit). This seemed to indicate a two-dimensional matrix. It was then noticed that there were also two sorts of sentences not involving sequences of sentence level tagmemes manifested by clauses, viz., particle sentences and clausal sentences (with the latter having the overall structure of a single clause – even though subordinate clauses might manifest clause level tagmemes within it). This left only two sentence types not readily relatable in a matrix: one type called a negative sentence, and the other an adversative sentence. But the negative sentence is itself an adversative sentence of an implicit variety (i.e. without an explicit adversative conjunction 'but'). The so-called adversative sentence had been considered to be problematical because the sprawling, elaborated structures seen in some examples seemed to constitute something on the order of a paragraph. Eventually the following matrix was posited, with five orders differentiated as to SIMPLE, CONDITIONAL, SEQUENCE, QUOTATION, and ADVERSATIVE, and with two series: (a) a series characterized by considerable internal cohesion of sentence structure; and (b) a series characterized by lesser internal cohesion:

	Simple	Conditional	Sequence	Quotation	Adversative
(a)	Particle	General	Closely-knit	Indirect	Implicit (Negative)
(b)	Clausal	Contrary to fact	Loosely-knit	Direct	Explicit

Trique sentence types (sentence proper, not colon) are accommodated best within three matrices. One matrix of two by four structure (with one lacuna) accommodates types of colloquy and monologue sequence sentences:

	Colloquy	Sequence
Clausal, more elaborated	Formal	Monologue B
Clausal, less elaborated	Cohortative	Monologue A
Phrasal structure	Particle B	Monologue title
Word structure	Particle A	

In the above matrix, formal colloquy is the structure mentioned in 15.1.; it contrasts with cohortative which is less formal and less elaborated. Particle B and A are discussed in 14.2. Monologue sequence B is discussed in 14.1. and 15.3.; the contrasting mono- logue sequence A lacks preposed temporal margin and has a more restricted choice of conjunction. Monologue title sentence is de- scribed in 15.1.

Trique interrogative, quotation, and conditional sentences are accommodated within a three by two matrix:

	Interrogative	Quotation	Conditional
More elaborate	Purpose question	Direct quotation	General condition
Less elaborate	Content question	Indirect quotation	Specific condition

Trique interrogative sentences are discussed in 14.7. Direct quota- tion permits a much larger and more complex quoted sequence than does indirect quotation. One Trique conditional type sentence is presented in 14.1.

Finally, three remaining Trique sentence types are accommodated within a one dimensional matrix (for the comparative, see 14.1.):

Alternative	Permissive	Comparative

14.7. Inspect the posited matrix or matrices for (a) con- firmation of sentence types already posited and (b) clues as to possible further types.

Thus, in setting up the Zoque matrix a decision was made to retain the adversative sentence (using the particle 'but') in spite of its rambling structure. Since series (b) in the Zoque sentence matrix seems to be characterized by sentence structures with less internal cohesion (witness the loosely-knit sequence sentence and the direct quotation that can include a paragraph or discourse), this adversative sentence no longer stands structurally isolated.

In the setting up of the second Trique sentence matrix a discovery was made that Trique interrogative sentences were of two varieties. One variety of a fairly straightforward nature involves preposing an interrogative content word (such as a^4mq^4 'when', yu^3h 'where', da^3h 'how') in a clause or colon, or preposing $a^3w\underline{i}^3$ 'who', $n\underline{u}^4h\ w\cdot\underline{i}^3$ 'what' to a relative clause or colon: $a^3w\underline{i}^3\ zi^{21}\ nga^4\ gq^3\mathcal{P}q^{34}h\ re^5\mathcal{P}$ 'whom did you go with?' ($zi^{21}\ nga^4\ gq^3\mathcal{P}q^{34}h\ re^5\mathcal{P}$ 'he with whom you went' is a relative clause). But another variety of interrogative preposes $n\underline{u}^{34}h\ w\cdot\underline{i}^3\ zi^3\ wa^3h\ ni^4$ 'why is it that...' ($n\underline{u}^4h\ w\cdot\underline{i}^3$ 'what is', $zi^3\ wa^3h$ 'that goes', ni^4 'and'), and thus has a more involved structure.

15. ANALYTICAL PROCEDURES FOR SENTENCE LEVEL TAGMEMES

In that sentence structures typically have fewer component tagmemes per emic type than do structures on lower levels, the problem of separating similar but distinct tagmemes within a sentence type is less acute. In this section we present, therefore, not suspect pairs of tagmas with criteria for analysis but rather a list of possible identifying-contrastive features of sentence level tagmemes. Although some of these features have already been mentioned in preceding sections we present them here in summary. This summary list (15.1.) is followed by procedures for recognizing repeat sequence of the same sentence level tagmeme (15.2.) and for separation of a complex sentence level tagmeme from a sequence of two such tagmemes (15.3.).

15.1. The following is a list of some identifying-contrastive features of sentence level tagmemes:

(1) Word types and root classes manifesting sentence level tagmemes not manifested by clauses.

PARTICLES: Particles which contain extra-systemic phonemes may constitute different tagmemes (and syntagmemes) from particles which contain phonemes in general use. Cf. English $o?o$, t^c, $t^c!!$ Trique $m^2?m^4$ 'no'; m^{53} 'yes' and a^3fi^2 'don't tell me!' (syllabic nasals and f do not occur elsewhere in Trique), also Trique-Mixtec bilabial trill for calling chickens.

A formal colloquy Trique sentence terminates with four tagmemes which may be termed: terminal temporal, terminal verb, emotional coloring, and vocative. Terminal temporal is manifested by one of two particles: $ga^5?$ 'yet, more', or na^3 'still'. Emotional coloring is manifested by a class of ten particles:[4] $(na^3)m\underline{i}^3$ 'counter-suggestion' often 'dubitative', $m\underline{a}^3h$ 'negative', $ni^2?$, $\underline{u}^2?$ 'interrogative', $n\underline{a}^3h$ 'asseverative', $nda^3r\underline{u}^4?$ 'despondent, wistful', $(za^3)d\varrho^3h$ 'suggestion', sometimes 'apologetic suggestion', $ve?e^5$ 'uncertain' (?), a^3 'mildly asseverative', za^5h 'cheerful, in accord', ni^4 'cheerful', sometimes 'exhortative' or 'promisory'. The other two tagmemes, terminal verb and vocative are manifested by more involved structures not relevant here.

CONJUNCTIONS are typically of importance to sentence structure. Section 15.3. discusses the problem as to when a conjunction patterns as part of a clause manifesting a sentence level tagmeme and when it patterns as manifesting a sentence level tagmeme in its own right.

NOUNS ACTING AS VOCATIVE (whether or not with a specific vocative structure) frequently figure in sentence level slots. In classical languages vocatives had characteristic case endings. In Trique, kinship terms used as vocatives carry intonation contours (not tone as such) which set them apart from all other word structures. These vocatives occur in one variety of nonclausal sentence and as the closing tagmeme in the formal colloquy sentence mentioned above.

(2) Phrase types and classes manifesting sentence level tagmemes not manifested by clauses.

Thus, Pickett describes "Non-clause independent sentence type 2" as consisting of a content question introducer slot (such as 'who', 'what', 'when', 'which') followed by a sentence base manifested by a noun phrase or by an independent pronoun expression, e.g. $u^!nǎ$ $^!bi\text{?}ku$ $^!wi\text{?}ini$ $kě$ 'where (is) that little dog!' ($u^!nǎ$ 'where', $^!bi\text{?}ku$ 'dog', $^!wi\text{?}ini$ 'little', $kě$ 'that').

In Trique a monologue title sentence consists of a noun phrase similar in structure to the item possessor phrase but with the following peculiarities: pseudo-item is manifested by $zi^3\text{-}gwe^4ntu^4$ 'a story of', and pseudo-possessor is manifested not only by noun phrase and relative sentence but by temporal clause as well (and thus has a broader manifesting class than the possessor of the item-possessor phrase).

CONJUNCTIVE PHRASES, as well as conjunctions, may manifest sentence level tagmemes. Thus, there is a sentence type in Trique (monologue sequence B) which consists of ± temporal margin (manifested by a subordinate clause introduced by nga^{43} 'when' ± sentence conjunction$_1$ + sentence base (manifested by certain clauses or colons). But sentence conjunction$_1$ is manifested not only by the conjunction ni^4 'and' but by the conjunctive phrases nga^{43} ni^4 'then-and'; and we^2 dq^3 ni^4 'so-then-and' (which are expansions of ni^4 'and' by adding preposed elements.)

(3) Clauses manifesting a given sentence level tagmeme may be (a) restricted as to type, (b) restricted as to internal structure within a type; (c) restricted as to lexical selection of some clause level tagmeme within a type.

(a) Thus, while Trique has four independent clause types, many colon level tagmemes are restricted in that they may be manifested by only clause types 1 and 2 (transitive and intransitive clauses). But the identification tagmeme of the assertion-identification colon is manifested only by clause type 4 (equative clause):

$a^3\text{?}nq^{35}\text{?}$ ngo^4 zi^{21} dq^3h $w\cdot i^3$ zi^3 ni^3ka^{34} $re^5\text{?}$ 'is-sick a certain man he's your husband.'

In this example, the clause $a^3\text{?}nq^{35}\text{?}$ ngo^4 zi^{21} dq^3h 'a certain man is sick' manifests assertion tagmeme while the balance of the colon manifests identification tagmeme and is a clause of type 4 (equative). In an effect cause sentence, however, effect tagmeme may be manifested not only by clause types 1 and 2 but by clause type 3 (meteorological):

$ga^3mq^{35}\textit{?}$ $gi^3\textit{?}ya^3h$ $yq^3\textit{?}qhq^{43}$
'rained   made   God'   i.e.'God caused it to rain'

$ga^3mq^{35}\textit{?}$ 'rained' is a meteorological clause (subjectless) and manifests effect tagmeme.

(b) Several Trique colon types contain tagmemes manifested by clauses restricted in various ways as to internal structure. For example, emphasis tagmeme of the emphasis-affirmation colon is manifested by a nuclear clause$_2$ (i.e. an intransitive clause consisting of nothing more than predicate and subject). Furthermore (anticipating discussion of restriction c below), the predicate of this nuclear clause$_2$ must be manifested by we^2 'lo, it is...', ze^2 'lo, it isn't', or ni^3ta^4h 'there isn't any' as in the sentence we^2 dq^{21} $w \cdot \textit{į}^3$ $\check{z}u^3h$ 'lo it is my animal' (dq^{21} 'my animal' is a pivot simultaneously manifesting subject of we^2 'lo it is', and subject of $w \cdot \textit{į}^3$ 'copulative'; $\check{z}u^3h$ 'animal'). Purpose tagmeme of a behaviour-purpose colon (cf. 14.3.) is manifested by clause$_1$ or clause$_2$ but the predicate tagmeme of the clause manifesting purpose must be in punctiliar aspect and anticipatory mood for all verbs inflected for aspect and mood. Cause tagmeme of an effect-cause colon (also exemplified under 14.3.) is manifested by a clause$_1$ with predicate tagmeme manifested by $\textit{?}ya^3h$ 'do, make'. Furthermore, the clause manifesting cause tagmeme is restricted in that, although $\textit{?}ya^3h$ is a transitive verb and regularly occurs with a goal, the goal is never found in such a clause manifesting cause (the effect clause functions as the LOGICAL, but not the grammatical goal). Audition tagmeme of a verbalization-audition colon is similarly restricted in that, although manifested by a clause$_1$ containing the transitive verb $gu^3n\ddot{\imath}^3$ 'hear', no goal may occur in the clause: $ga^3ta^{34}h$ zi^3 $gu^3n\ddot{\imath}^{21}$ 'he said to me' ($ga^3ta^{34}h$ 'said', zi^3 'he', $gu^3n\ddot{\imath}^{21}$ 'heard-I'). Furthermore, the verb $gu^3n\ddot{\imath}^3$ 'hear' is always punctiliar (the continuative aspect is $u^3n\ddot{\imath}^3$). Conversely, there is another Trique colon type, the attitude-direction colon, which contains direction tagmeme manifested by clause$_1$ restricted in two ways: (a) its predicate must be manifested by $ni^3\textit{?}i^3$ 'seeing' in the continuative aspect (the punctiliar aspect is $gi^3ni^3\mathit{?}i^3$); and (b) a goal must occur (normally in Trique transitive clauses the goal is nuclear but optional, in that it may be omitted granted sufficient context). Thus: $a^3\mathit{?}mq^3$ ru^3wa^{23} $re^5\mathit{?}$ $ni^3\mathit{?}i^2$ $re^5\mathit{?}$ $mq^3\mathit{?}q^{21}$ 'You're angry at me' ($a^3\mathit{?}mq^3$ ru^3wa^{23} 'angry', $re^5\mathit{?}$ 'you', $ni^3\mathit{?}i^3$ 'seeing' (stem tones become ^{32} before $re^5\mathit{?}$), $mq^3\mathit{?}q^{21}$ 'me').

The Zoque contrary to fact condition (13.4.) illustrates a sentence type both tagmemes of which are manifested by clauses restricted in respect to a nonnuclear feature, viz. both clauses must contain a temporal tagmeme manifested by enclitic *-na?ŋ* 'past time'.

Restriction (c) – restriction of lexical selection within a clause manifesting some sentence level tagmeme – has been illustrated several places in the above paragraphs.

(4) Included sentence structures may manifest sentence level tagmemes. The types of sentence manifesting such a sentence level tagmeme constitute therefore an identifying-contrastive feature of the tagmeme they manifest.

Many Trique sentence types contain tagmemes manifested not only by certain clause types but by certain colon types (lower level sentence structures) as well. Notice the example under 15.3., where sentence base tagmeme in the monologue sequence B sentence is manifested by a verbalization-audition colon ga^5ta^5 gu^3ni^2 $re^5\mathit{?}$ 'will-tell-I hear you', i.e. 'I'll tell you'. Precise identification of which colon types may manifest various tagmemes in Trique sentences leads to a better delineation of the identifying-contrastive features of each tagmeme which they manifest.

Direct quotation sentences in many languages have a quoted tagmeme which may be manifested by any independent sentence in the language. Furthermore, in many languages an indefinitely long sequence of sentences may manifest quoted tagmeme. Although this amounts to the inclusion of a paragraph or discourse within a sentence, this is no stranger than the inclusion of a clause within a phrase. It seems to be a fact of language structure that while syntagmemes on a given level typically contain tagmemes manifested by syntagmemes of lower levels, nevertheless those tagmemes may be manifested by syntagmemes from a higher level. Where such feedback from a higher level occurs, it serves to distinguish the tagmeme so manifested from other sentence level tagmemes.

(5) Sentence level tagmemes may be further distinguished as to relative order within the sentence. Thus, the first two sentence schemes given in 13.4. are characterized by linear ordering of tagmemes in the order given. This order is, therefore, an identifying-contrastive feature of each tagmeme. But the third scheme given in that section (Zoque contrary to fact conditional sentence) permits an optional ordering of tagmemes in reverse sequence to that given in the formula. In this third sentence type, linear ordering of sentence level tagmemes is nondistinctive.

15.2. Postulate possible multiple occurrence of some sentence level tagmemes where so indicated in the data.

In Chatino a reason sentence has the following structure: $+$Reason ($+$Hinge$_2$: $ko\Omega^2$ $t\check{s}a\Omega^2$ 'that's why' $+$Outcome)^2 Superscript ^{2} indicates that (Hinge$_2$ $+$Outcome) can occur twice in the same sentence.

REASON SENTENCE

$\check{s}a^2nu^3$ $\check{s}lyu^{32}$ $ne\Omega^2$ mo^3 $kino^4$ su^2 la^3 $mbre^4$, ($=$ reason)
'when turn   they machine base   wire'
(When they turn the machine at the base of the wire)

$ko\Omega^2$ $t\check{s}a\Omega^2$ ($=$ hinge$_2$) $ne^1 la^3$ $mbre^4$, ($=$ outcome) $ko\Omega^2$ $t\check{s}a\Omega^2$
'that-is why   sounds wire'   'that-is why
(that is why)   (the wire hums)   (that is why)

($=$ hinge$_2$) $ngiya^{43}$ $kw\underset{.}{e}^2$ la^3 $mbre^4$ ($=$ outcome)
          going   loudly   wire'
          (the wire hums loudly)

A Chatino purpose sentence has the following structure: $+$Setting ($+$Hinge$_1$: $t\check{s}a\Omega^2$ 'in order that' $+$Purposive)^n. Superscript^n here indicates that ($+$Hinge$_1$ $+$Purposive) may occur an indefinite number of the times in the same sentence. Although in the present data no examples occur with more than four purposive clauses, it seems that in principle we have here an open structure permitting the generating of a sentence of monstrous length were any Chatino speaker in a sufficiently frivolous mood to do so:

nsiʔya¹ neʔ³   msu³⁴   ʔị¹ neʔ³ wta³⁴ (= setting)
'calling persons servants of his   cattle'
(The people that are their servants are calling the cattle)

tšaʔ²   (= hinge₁) *šoʔ¹*   *suʔwa⁴³ neʔ² ʔị³   niʔ³*
'in-order-that   will-collect will-put they them inside
in order to   (collect them together in the corrals of

lyoʔo³² rantšu⁴ ʔị¹ ʔị³   (= purposive) *tšaʔ²*   (= hinge₁)
in-corral ranch of theirs'   'in-order-that
their ranches)   in order to

kulo⁴³   *neʔ² styiʔ² ʔị³*   (= purposive) *tšaʔ²*
will-draw-out they milk of-theirs'   in-order-that
      (milk them)   in order to

(= hinge₁) *tyiʔo³²*   *kšu³⁴   ʔị¹ neʔ³*   (= purposive)
    will-cause-to-emerge cheese of person's'
            (make cheese)

tšaʔ²   (= hinge₁) *tsa³²   hwiʔ⁴³ neʔ² lo³ kiyaʔ³²*
'in-order-that   will-go sell   they in market'
so that   (they can sell it in the market)

(= purposive)

15.3. Look for sequences of sentence level tagmas that are suspect of being not two distinct sentence level tag-memes but only one sentence level tagmeme manifested by a lower level syntagmeme, which would in this case probably be some sort of clause structure. Analyze this suspect sequence as constituting one sentence level tag-meme whenever overall tactical considerations suggest such an analysis.

Consider again the Trique sentence type (monologue sequence B)

mentioned under 15.1. and exemplified in the following sentence:
nga^{43} $na^4ni^3ka^{34}h$ re^5P nga^{43} ni^4 ga^5ta^5 gu^4ni^2 re^5P 'When return-you then and will-tell-I hear you'. (nga^{43} 'when', $na^4ni^3ka^{34}h$ 'will return', nga^{43} ni^4 'then and' ga^5ta^5 'will-tell-I', gu^4ni^2 re^5P 'will-hear you'). How many sentence level tagmemes should be posited for this sentence type? Thus, $na^4ni^3ka^{34}h$ re^5P 'will-return you' is a readily isolable sequence having the structure of clause$_2$ (intransitive clause), while ga^5ta^5 gu^3ni^2 re^5P 'I'll tell you (will-tell-I, hear you)' is isolable as the colon structure described above as verbalization-audition. But where do the conjunctions fit in? Have we a first conjunction tagmeme manifested by nga^{43} 'when' and a second conjunction tagmeme manifested by nga^{43} ni^4 'then and'? This at first seems plausible in that nga^{43} 'when' ... nga^{43} ni^4 'when and' seem to co-occur together in the same sentence while $nda^{43}...da^{43}P$ nga^{43} zi^3 'until ... until when that' seem to co-occur in other sentences. But there is considerable to be argued in favor of making only the second conjunction tagmeme a sentence level tagmeme, while relegating the tagmeme manifested by nga^{43} 'when' and nda^{43} 'until' to the clause level. To begin with, nga^{43} and nda^{43} never introduce sentences as such but only subordinate clauses (or subordinate colons), while nga^{43} ni^4 'and then' and $da^{43}P$ nga^{43} zi^3 'and then' often introduce sentences: nga^{43} ni^4 $gq^3Pq^{34}h$ zi^3 'Then (at that time) he went off' and $da^{43}P$ nga^{43} zi^3 $gq^3Pq^{34}h$ zi^3 'Then (after some previous activity) he went off'. Furthermore, nga^{43} and nda^{43} are simple, nonexpandable conjunctions, while nga^{43} ni^4 and $da^{43}P$ nga^{43} zi^3 are phrasal expansions of simpler conjunctions introducing sentences (see conjunctive phrases under 15.1.).

In brief, both in terms of distribution and internal structure, nga^{43} 'where' and nda^{43} 'until' seem to be distinct from nga^{43} ni^4 'and then' and $da^{43}P$ nga^{43} zi^3 'and then'. Furthermore, it seems that an introducer tagmeme properly belongs tagmemically on the level of that which it introduces rather than on the next higher level. A case in point is the analysis of prepositions. Prepositions are commonly considered to introduce certain phrase types (prepositional phrases) and to fill a phrase level slot; they are not considered to constitute clause level tagmemes linking one part of the clause to another part of the clause. So it seems parallel to consider subordinate conjunctions to fill a clause level slot rather than to fill a sentence level slot (cf. 1.0.). It then follows that conjunctions and conjunctive phrases which introduce sentences as such (even if a subordinate clause may be optionally preposed) manifest sentence level tagmemes.

Thus, our Trique sentence given above may be analyzed as having the following structure: temporal margin tagmeme manifested by nga^{43} $na^4ni^3ka^{34}h$ $re^5\text{?}$ 'when you return'; sentence conjunction manifested by nga^{43} ni^4 'and then'; sentence base manifested by the colon ga^5ta^5 gu^3ni^2 $re^5\text{?}$ 'I'll tell you'.

This analysis entails our setting up a subordinate clause type for Trique (2.6.). Nevertheless, the overall tactical considerations just stated seem to indicate that it is better further to complicate clause structure at this point than to attempt to dispose of the problem on the sentence level.

16. CONCLUDING PROCEDURES FOR SENTENCE LEVEL ANALYSIS

16.1. Residues should now be reexamined in the light of the analysis of sentence level syntagmemes and tagmemes obtained by the above procedures. Some by-passed sentences may prove to be intricate nestings of sentence type within sentence type. Other residues may indicate the necessity of positing one or more new sentence types.

Thus in the analysis of Zoque sentence types, there were certain sentences containing *ke* 'that, to the effect that' which were unaccounted for. Furthermore, although conditional sentences containing *ho?ka* 'if' had been analyzed, there were other sentences in which *ho?ka* did not seem to mean 'if' but was apparently synonymous with the *ke* particle just mentioned. In fact, in many such sentences *ke* and *ho?ka* were interchangeable. All fell into place when it was recognized that these various examples could be considered to be indirect quotations (see 14.3.).

16.2. Write a brief summary sketch of sentence level

syntagmemes and tagmemes. For each sentence type and each constituent tagmeme give identifying-contrastive features.

16.3. Check rapidly the above description of sentence structure against a larger corpus. Look only for data which adds to, clarifies, or modifies the description.

16.4. Revise the description to account for the data of the fuller corpus; write up in more complete and elegant form.

BIBLIOGRAPHY

Church, Clarence and Katherine, "The Jacaltec Noun Phrase", *Mayan Studies I, Linguistic Series of the Summer Institute of Linguistics* 5.159-70 (1960).

Cox, Doris, "Candoshi Verb Inflection", *International Journal of American Linguistics* 23.129-49 (1957).

Delgaty, Colin C., "Tzotzil Verb Phrase Structure, *Mayan Studies I, Linguistic Series of the Summer Institute of Linguistics* 5.32-126 (1960).

Eachus, Frances, "K'ekchi' Clause Structure" (unpublished paper).

Elliott, Ray, "Ixil (Mayan) Clause Structure, *Mayan Studies I, Linguistic Series of the Summer Institute of Linguistics* 5.127-54 (1960).

Elson, Benjamin and Velma Pickett, *An Introduction to Morphology and Syntax* (Santa Ana, California, Summer Institute of Linguistics, 1962).

Engel, Ralph, and Robert E. Longacre, "Syntactic Matrices in Ostuacan Zoque", *International Journal of American Linguistics* 29.331-44 (1963).

Flores, Francisco G., *A Contrastive Analysis of Selected Clause Types in Cebuano and English*, (University of Michigan Ph.D. dissertation, 1962).

Fox, David, "Quiché Clause Structure" (unpublished paper).

Hockett, Charles, "Potawatomi Syntax", *Language* 15.235-48 (1939).

Hoijer, H., "The Apachean Verb", *International Journal of American Linguistics* 11.193-203; 12.1ff., 51ff., 14.247ff.; 15.12ff. (1945-9).

Longacre, Robert E., "From Tagma to Tagmeme in Biblical Hebrew", *A Guillermo Townsend en el Vigésimoquinto Aniversario del Instituto Lingüístico de Verano* (Mexico City, 1961).

——, "String Constituent Analysis", *Language* 36.63-88 (1960).

McKaughan, Howard P., *The Inflection and Syntax of Maranao Verbs* (Manila, 1958).

Mohiyud-Din, Muhammad, "The Bengali Noun Phrase" (unpublished paper).

Pickett, Velma B., *Hierarchical Structure of Isthmus Zapotec* (= *Language Dissertation No. 56*) (Baltimore, 1960).

Pike, Kenneth L., "Dimensions of Grammatical Constructions", *Language* 38.221-44 (1962).

——, *Language in Relation to a Unified Theory of the Structure of Human Behavior* (Glendale, Vol. I: 1954, Vol. II: 1955, Vol. III: 1960). To be republished soon as one volume in revised form by Mouton and Co., The Hague.

Pride, Kitty "Chatino Syntax "(unpublished paper scheduled to appear in the *Linguistic Series of the Summer Institute of Linguistics*).

Shell, Olive A. Cashibo II: "Grammemic Analysis of Transitive and Intransitive Verb Patterns", *International Journal of American Linguistics* 23.179-218 (1957).

Vincent, Alex, and Vincent, Lois, "Introductory Notes on Tairora Verb Morphology and Syntax", *Studies in New Guinea Linguistics* by members of the Summer Institute of Linguistics, New Guinea Branch (= *Oceania Linguistic Monographs No. 6*) (1962), 4-27.

Waterhouse, Viola, "Independent and Dependent Sentences", *International Journal of American Linguistics* 29.45-54 (1963).

——, *The Grammatical Structure of Oaxaca Chontal* (= *Publication Nineteen of the Indiana University Research Center in Anthropology, Folklore, and Linguistics*) (1962).

West, John D., "Notes on Mikasuki (Seminole) Action Clause Types" (unpublished paper).

Wise, Mary Ruth, "Six Levels of Structure in Amuesha (Arawak) Verbs", *International Journal of American Linguistics* 29.132-52 (1963).

Wonderly, William L., *Zoque: Phonemics and Morphology, International Journal of American Linguistics* 17.1-9, 105-23, 137-61, 235-51; 18.35-48, 189-202 (1951, 1952).

Zvelebil, Kamil, "How to Handle the Structure of Tamil", *Archiv Orientální* 30.116-42 (1962).

INDEX